Amidst the Chilling Storm

FRANK KARAN

Ordering Information:

Prime Seven Media
518 Landmann St.
Tomah City, WI 54660

Printed in the United States of America

TABLE OF CONTENTS

PREFACE

Amidst the chilling storm was inspired by my father
Because he was always telling me tales of his early
Life as a shepherd boy!

Beauty rises above the weeds, was inspired by my mother
As she always looks simply elegant and stunningly great
And for instilling in me good taste and proper values!

I would also like to thank Trikki, the star of the
Wrestling show Ignition for the photo for Champion

Movie martial arts, action stars

Jean Claude Van Damme for streetfighter
Chuck Norris, for Win Every Fight

Frank Karan for the poems

Couldn't Be Unfaithful
Fooling the Fool
Tickling Schism

To the readers:

Wishing all the best.

-Frank Karan

ABYSS ATLAS

Spider spider, on the paper wall
Be careful not to slip then fall
Into a large bowl of boiling porridge
Scolding hot too hot, then fly cannot

Roam in the air n'drivel everywhere
Be aware to safely land, down there
Don't let chains bind you're scintling walk
Leave behind your rusty lust, it's not just

Don't be distressed by maiden's vows
Steer a course sailing forever proud
If not enchanted anyhow there lies a
Crypt of vicious vipers, for you now

Slight and short compile to naught
Born too soon gone for noon; death
Greets it's victims, with a scarry toll
It feels the greed to win a virgin soul

Cruising the abyss atlas is the epitome
To coercively foresee revitable destiny
So be weary of pivotal travels and ails
And be thankful only to where you avail

ACHES CRY

Pain is lurking in n'all around
Seizing victims on random round
Stumbling blocks make ladders larger
Can you contribute any major charger?

Children swing on swings, while siren's
Wail in the wind, laughter aches and aches
Cry; Shall we let it slip on by? Or adjust
Harness sadle whilst droving thirsty cattle

Factories ooze out their venomous plough
Gushy slime intoxicates the clear ground
Adding refuse to greenhouse's peer mound
Our atmosphere can't fortify major bound

Don't cripple my heart with your radioactive
Chart. Please have pity for my swelling part
Don't crucify my sincere art; or the passion
Of a mighty blood flowing: terricolous start

Looking around do you see? Can you see?
Is there anything that you really would
Like to be?. How can we eradicate hate
Envy n'greed from every race and creed?

AD HOC VERB

Which is better to lie or cry
I ask of you to tell me why?
I awoke as you spoke of the
Mambo sun, it's fiery rays

Were no joke, believe me son
It's barren heat weighed a ton
As i made my escape to oasis tarn
Guns, planes n'army trains dissolve

With rust, bandits of darkness shift
Into top gear; their nocturnal fear!
Surmise surprise get the lies out of
Your eyes, classic images don't burn

As wax, if you prefer then make tracks
Axes and saws are tools used to achieve
A formidable score, is it worth yielding
For? Ipso-facto; there must be much more

Sex appeal teases everyone for a spill
Is that a viable trill or a cheap ill?
Chiselled in granite we looked superb
Everything that we did was ad hoc verb

Risque is my plan of malady divorce, from
The mammoth social sour of repeat discourse
Stomped on by a bleeding mad bull, dragged
Through arid plains of prickly cactus scrub

Debris scorpion n'snake, i tilly-vally
We pivot in shifting sand and lose our rake
I see a mirage; it's a scumble mistake
I feel the rubble splatter, it's earthquake

ALL YOU ACT

The world exploded in my face
As it was pelted magma pace
The closest encounter of your
Life yielded so much strife

Whilst directing dangerous scene
You couldn't participate obscene
You only thought you'd direct the
Role but you ended up protagonist

Whole: as pretentious bossoms
Bestowed inveigling your mode
Sarcasm was a puddle because you
Were too frail to strode shuttle

Having held it's debut on stage two
It was cursed unrehearsed, only one
Act it played staking inaugural way
Academy award winner; mega money filler

Tinsel town spinner! Can i take you out
To dinner you stunning sidewalk sinner?
You'll sign a pact n'use ten fold tact
Renumerating epenthesis of all you act

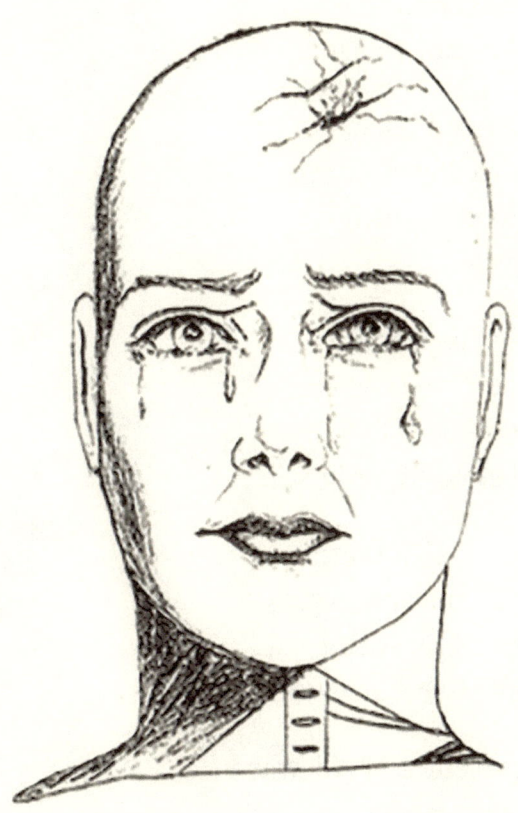

AGNOSTIC ANDROID

I don't want to be left alone
Tired, hungry, away from home
Scolded by the scorching torch
I wish to quickly run ablaze

Into a safe sheltered haze
Where pure trickling streams
Sparkle in clear days, little
Hummingbirds glisten in gaze

My hard harvest is promptly due
Only to be wasted on bills cue!
I seek to be exalted; not vaulted
In this faulted skyscraper jungle

Whilst in it where all a bundle
Clashes, crashes, houses, gases
Buildings higher sire; surmount
To metal mount: Babel account!

Endeavouring relentlessly forward
Searching for sum sincere emotion
In a throwaway society we cannot
Afford to hackaway it's variety!

Is this recent modern living?
Or future giving, listen closely
To our misgiving, agnostic android
Can't be a part of human forgiving

AMIDST THE CHILLING STORM

Encircling myself in full captivating bliss
I try to shield my veins from nature's fury
The elements are opposed to any human glory
Do i sense victory? Or another bitter story

My misery depends on my efforts alone
The wrath of the gods are upon me now
Zeus throws his lightning thunder down
Clamping hard, on the mudsoaked ground

Laying down amidst the chilling storm
My heart beats raw like a diamond saw
I solemnly vow that i won't give in, to
Dreadful demons and atrocious evil sins

A burning passion heckles n'rages my skin
Lord give me shelter from the biting cold
Come and guide me and my flock of sheep
For i am yielding in mental traffic, to

The enticing tunes, of witches n'elves
The howling of wolves sends a tingling
Fear into my blood stiffening my thud
I must hurry before i sink in the mud

The ferocity of darkness is well renowned
Forests lush out their obnoxious rebound
Goblins dance in the misty valleys below
The weird lust of the night leaves me low

AMUSE OUR FUSE

Very gently i blew soft wind thru your
Tangled wavy hair it lustered bouncing
Flair, you rose receptively against my
Bitter stare slipping on your black shoes

Whilst rattling underground, forgetting
Troubling sins, how was i then to know
That i would ·fall in love with you and
Your fears would not let you stay then

You'd run away; if i was to carefully hold
You in the morning after we slept and asked
How do you feel? Would you think i was merely
Mocking or cocking your pit, are you confused?

Do you think that we used our bodies just to
Amuse our fuse? Yesterday's news! I only ever
Wanted to spice up your flavoured life n'steal
Away the ugly vice, isn't that nice? I'v always

Sailed out on many a sea just to see what i
Could see, so what did i see? At the end of
This journey I'll be done; my destination
Will be one, then you'll know you've won!

ANIMATE YOUR MATE

It was back in time
When you were mine
The world did rhyme
But that was back in time

After all this slime
Can you really grind?
Do you still maintain
To be the one and only main?

Where is your fortune?
What have you gained?
Animate your mate to a
Renewed congenial frenzied state!

Is that truly your intention
Or just a cheap prevention?
Wipe away those bitter silly tears
Which have bought chill for many years

My heart is like the depleting ozone layer
I feel like a mutation of CFC trapped in an
Aerosol can, I can't take much more of this
Ultra-violet light it's skin cancer bright!

Don't drag along a heavy heart with a worn
Slippery patchy part, integrate the sifting
Cart; rejuvenate the old lubricating mart by
Animating your mate to an exciting fiesta start

APHORISMS

The cost of this philosophy is free
Just exercise it cautiously, results
Will follow fostering a new tomorrow!

Study good, study right, do your homework n'sleep tight
Memory will play it's part; tomorrow you'll stay smart!

Don't work below your capacity if you want to reach above it
Never depend upon commercial ratings for your own happiness
A woman and a man should help eachother the best they can
Everything is open if you let it, the key is to get it
Anything can be finer yet everything can't be perfect
Appreciate what you have and not what you desire
Arrogance and pride make us narrow minded blind
The more you experience the more you understand
The breaks are there but you have to take them
The bigger the opponent the bigger the target
There is more than one answer to one question
Everyone regrets something but not everything
Opportunities come and go; so don't be slow
You have to drink your milk before it sours
Success is diffusive like fame is elusive
We must make the most of what we've got
If your not born with it, develop it

Desperate people do desperate things
The teacher is an advanced student
Behind an answer lies a question
One can see all but grasp little
Two halves don't make a whole
Offense is the best defense
Technology is never ending
Imagination is infinite
No venture no adventure
Talent can be nurtured
Science is expanding
Love is ecstatic
Life is a paradox
Knowledge is power
A risk may be brisk
Anyone can influence
Business is sporadic
Politics is sarcastic
Empires rise then fall
You only have one body
You only live one life

Inspiration is erratic
Don't spit as you speak
Hippocrates are pathetic
Don't step on a minefield
Diplomacy is hectic shrewd
If you don't fight you lose
Happiness comes from within
Negativity breeds negativity

Technique requires commitment
Everyone has responsibilities
A leader needs to be followed
Everyone is good at something
There's always something to do
There's a reason for everything
Innovators create imitators copy
Never underestimate your opponent
Without wisdom power may turn sour
For every action there's a reaction
Time is valuable; so don't waste it
If your negative switch to positive
Your mind tells your body what to do
Without an audience the actor is bare
You don't always get what you pay for

There's always something new to learn
There's always a higher level to reach
Success is there for those who want it
Positive thoughts spur positive action
A legend has to be renewed and renowned
If you can't pay cash; can you afford it?
If the boat rocks then adjust the balance
There's always a balance and an inbalance
The cure may be deadlier than the disease
Winners never quit and quitters never win
Everyone has strong points and weak points
If there's a way in then there's a way out
Do you judge people by what they say or do?
If you're not on top then you must be below

Proper preparation prevents poor performance
You don't know what you can do till you do it
When faced with complexity turn to simplicity
If you can change your point of view so can i
If it's not on the page it's not on the stage
It's not what you say it's the way you say it
You can't have everything but you can sure try
If you believe in what you do then see it thru
If you want to succeed then don't aim at defeat

It's not what you know; it's what you do with it
You've got to know what you want before you get it
It's not the size of the man but the man in the size
If you fight fire with fire you create a bigger blaze
A theory needs to be tried n'tested before it's proven
If you look at people that do less then you'll do less
Would you prefer a little of a lot or a lot of a little?
If you don't have a destination then you won't reach one

When you achieve your goal; What pain lurks in your soul?
You cannot earnestly expect to master something overnight
Once you've learnt something you can use it again n'again
You can always put an old picture into a new picture frame
If you don't challenge something then you won't surpass it
If you don't do anything then you shouldn't expect anything
You have to distinguish the dolphins from the hungry sharks
An instructor can only guide you but you have to do the rest
Tell me where you've been and I'll tell you where you're going
If you don't wish to stagnate then you should learn to advance
It doesn't matter how good you are there's always someone better
You have to drink from the other man's cup to sample his beverage

You have to realise your limitations if you wish to go beyond them
Everything has it's price and prize; If you want it you have to pay it
Anyone can be knocked down but it's what you do when you rise that counts
When you're on a good thing stick to it If you find something better switch to it

No matter who you are, or what you are, at all times appreciate, Respect and accept others for who they are and for what they are

AREN'T WE LOVERS ALL THE WAY

You couldn't feel any better
Any better than this
Any better than now
You can scream, wow

Say what you will think
Of me, aloud and within
Vibrations are coursing
Vividly through my skin

When two hearts fuse
I just want to flash
When you're with another guy
I just wish to dash!

All of our warm actions
And every word, we call
Are directing us this way
And navigating love's ray

My heart is not only
A tank pumping blood
It's working overtime
Piping out the flood!

You are the vessel
Attached to my soul
Ascending us to an
Inspirational whole

Can you see my point?
Why run away?
Aren't we lovers
All the way?

AROMATHERAPY

Vivid aromatherapy enters our spleen
Flowering thoughts of affluent green
A sumptuous host metephysically keen
Aloud n'alive like you've never seen

Another chapter grazing the has been
Truntling meadows so fresh and clean
Dribbling drooling juices robust bean
A voluptuous murmur mesmerizing scene

Like an alchemist with element supreme
Peppermint is a cool antiseptic serene
Clay sage relieves sore throats, while
Cypress co-ordinates circulatory boats

In sickness and health it can boast
Soothing wealth like bomber stealth
Vivid aromatherapy enters our spleen
Flowering thoughts of affluent green

BARBARIAN SCREAM

A tyrant portrayed the darkest role
Shovelling humanity in Hell's hole
Thirsty, hungry with a biting pole
Wavering sensations of a heavy toll

Did he ever play with a doll?
Many wonder if he had a soul?
The savage race inhumanely sought
Knowledge; some excluded to abort

Why did they unleash they're deadly
Machine with a mad barbarian scream
Mental wielders, physical shielders
On sad apocalyptic horses they rode

Tractors towed, mankind bestowed
Money power ego, everything owed
Flashing a glittery satin heirloom
The entire planet shared the gloom

The shade vanished from the papaya
Fresh green flowing, fruity leaves
Only wilting bitter shedding reeds
Not redolent, in a summer's breeze

Masters of birth, heaven and earth
Spiritual healers, arms free wheelers
Must crystallize to end the bitter war
Which our forefathers bravely fought for

BATTLES RAGE PEOPLE DIE

Waiting in the wind with nothing to spin
This bachelor now lives alone; all alone
Humans n'birds play on Venetian squares
Armies as hard as tusks, tread anywhere

Pitiful plum am i, in cold Winter's eye
So take it easy gemester, for I'm no toy
Should you divorce my right to divorce?
From sickening thorns that bullet within

Battles rage and people die; Unburied
Battles rage and people die; Unloved
How is your scoff? Is it still bold?
Do decisions plague your inner mind?

Reality... Oh master of space and time
Can you help me lead a healthier life?
It's amazing what co-operation can do
If everyone put in the austere time

To scrub out the slime! Do you mind?

BEARS LIKE HONEY

Bears like honey
Like i like money
When I'm with you
Everything's sunny

You can make me sing
You can make me swing
You can cross the state
Then break my prostate

I don't need much time to
Vitalize the harum, fine
I'm tizzy like a grizzly
As you titilate your tit

Causing me to tenderly fit
Avoiding a scourging slit
Wasted all of my money
It wasn't quite funny

Coz you were my bunny
In delectable honey
Wrapped up like an
Egyptian mummy

Bears like honey
Like i like money
When I'm with you
Everything's sunny
    "HONEY"

BEAUTY RISES ABOVE THE WEEDS

I leave you; love so sweet
To steer a course complete
Hailstones hit hard the ground
Causing puddles to be found...

Beauty rises above the weeds
Remaining soft for all to see
Fearing pain is nothing more
Than the mind of the desolate poor

Sparkling rhythms of mental health
Help you see with greater wealth
Reflections of fantasies re-enter
My mind clouding clarity for a time

Obscuring all measure for treasure
Into the twilight i vaguely descend
Candle lit low, come near me friend
Reconcile your thoughts for an end

BECOME A PAIR

You're entitled to have a rapid raging pace
Just to be in this ferocious, amicable race
The Grand Prix is the place, where there's
No disgrace, just get up n'go, actual mace

Even though your tired eyes shine bright
And make me feel so comfortably right
They disintegrate all my reciprocal lies
Withering out my winsome phobic cries

All i really wanted was you
To stick by me and be true
Think of what we share
When we unite, become a pair

BEHIND HER VEIL

Why do you have to destroy
The love we did once enjoy
We only have one life to live
With peace and love we'll act

Without it we may get wacked
My ego exploded as your heart
Folded; into the emptiness of night
Jilting the day dwindling the light

Venus hirles herself behind her veil
So i cannot determine; what is real
How can i try to properly explain
When you look at me, with a flame

My heart humbly decides to kneal
Just to see what lies behind her veil
It must be something magical n'adventurously
Tragical, just to see the loveliness of her appeal

BE SOUND WITHOUT A SOUND

You cannot look at me
Straight in the eye so
You tell me a quick lie
Though physically we don't

Communicate mentally we'll
Participate, n'reciprocate
Why press your warm breast
Onto my lonely hairy chest

Disregard, all of the rest
Remember, what is the best
Please rise up to the test
So bounce like a golf ball

That gets beaten n'battered
Then lost then again found
Pound for pound, just be
Sound, without a sound

BITTER SLY

I love you but i don't know why
You hurt me, and i start to cry
That makes you feel pretty high
But i want you till the day i die

Without you; i just cannot get by
Why do you keep acting bitter sly
N'why do you still reject me? Why
Can't you at least; give me a try

BLACK HOLE

You make me come alive
So i bizz buzz the hive
Do we care to take five
Or just jump around jive

Your gun was only half cocked
As iran round the-blurry block
Beating the clock a nasty shock
I rushed in with blind eye mock

Bitterly dazing horribly grazing
The chick'in black shrieked when
I tumble freaked; speakeasy week
Power pole catapulted unfettered

In the dauntingly infinite black hole
Strategically i exceeded haggling role
Regimentally perturbing habitual toll
I'm now complacent to bury black hole

That imperiously repressed sojourn pole
The flag of truce which i bravely raised
Only half mast it knavery stays, as if in
A cast forever past humility leaves us fast

BOTHERED FOOL

I don't wish to criticize even ostracize
I don't mean to get caught in the middle
Or to play a decrepitating second fiddle
I'm just so intrigued with life's riddle

Why should you be embroiled in any sadness
Can't you find a way, to shake the madness
Near n'far; you'd always like to be a star
Bothered fool i pity your collapsing stool

Dangling upon the empty, rock hard pool
Every select section has some infection
You can't always expect total perfection
So how can you handle adverse rejection?

BRIGHTER HORIZON

I saw you getting extremely tired as you
Faced the troublesome fears with courage
A remedy for your ailment; was not to be
So i caringly said that you come with me

And there was so much more to see
Thus a brighter horizon for you n'me
You're ugly bitter fight was not in vain
Trying to find comfort from the savage pain

There was nothing lost but so much wealth to gain
If you gave me your heart, i could love you forever
We will paint new colours on the floating crimson sky
We can navigate to a peaceful hemisphere, tenderly high

BUFFERED IN BLISS

I was alcohol induced
When your love seduced
An empty bed and hangover
Were consequently produced

Our galaxy is like a rusty nail
Protruding it's ageing solidity
Through the cosmic cyber hail
I should never; feel so frail

Trawling on the animosity rail
Is there a deflection, for the
Latest venom chronic infection
I hope it won't have some wild

Contagious connection, or a mimickly
Derelict projection, my thoughts are
Still buffered in bliss, of when we
First touched n'passionately kissed

Your such a cute, lovable twist
That's why i can't resist, your
Frolicking laugh, it's like the
Frosty mist, buffered in bliss!

BURIED IN BLOOD
COVERED WITH MUD

In a collage of broken bodies
Rotting meat and smelly bone
Virgin soldiers lay in swamps
Buried in blood, covered with mud

Marrowless bones grind with grief
Melanin lips reveal the lust
Withered jaws can feel the crust
Come near me if you must!

Like childrens toys lost in slime
Swampy marshes erode their time
Insidious lakes possess the might
They try to numb; devour your right

While man swelters in the sand
Camels call it their oasis land
Sorrow bites into my chest
Ripping venom from my flesh

Scolding grains attack my skin
Incubating germs thrive within
Wielding flames ignite with spite
Seek forth the one and only plight

CAN I BE WITH YOU?

I wouldn't say I'm good
I wouldn't say I'm bad
I'd rather be dogmatic
Mad than simple sad

I don't want to feel
Like a worn out fad
Take a ride with me and
Shake the inhibition tree

Drown your doubt in the sea
So now you can be free
To spend your life with me!
How about the fee?

It's so simple to see
Tell me why without a lie
Tell me true without a clue
Can i be with you?

CAN YOU FEEL THIS HEART

Can you feel this heart? It loves you
Must you see these eyes? They're blue
when I'm with you i smokestack unwind
I unleash pleasure from quadrant find

Do you think of me in your soft bed
Or do you eat me as wholemeal bread
You've must have been pompously fed
Living in a dream where have i been

Splendid icy excitement i have seen
What an astronomical puzzling scene
A merriment of wonder all too preen
A kaleidoscope of astonishment keen

You're such a sweet talker, you can
Do anything; singing the right song
You can't go wrong, especially when
The arrangement is so concrete long

Don't ride the mystery bus with so
Much fuss, just get rid of the pus
There is no solace for my yearning
Baby for you, I'm barbecue burning

CANISTER YOUR DOMAIN

Plunging into the fiery abstruse lake
Not knowing what King's evil to await
Bubbles beguile their innocent troth
Truth surfaces amidst chilling froth

Franchise exists for those who summon
A better score, you gleam supreme with
Fresh esteem, stand proud amongst the
Craving crowd freakish freckles slough

So less, their misery you can not bless
Their flesh is embezzled in microscopic
Mess; the fallopian tube i must detest
It's a fallible fragmented jezz: chess

Condescending Charon glees at his fragile
Prey when he knows it's a dull, foolhardy
Frigid prank, so praise no-one in a dummy
Precarious world, predestination belies a

Musing guise of one precious preceptor who
Slinks at all, scherzo appears on the big
Chugging screen, churning out it's choler
Like a disease, Auntie Cilia perceived the

Gelatinous germane; White Heaven bewails
My vulnerable ail: Black Hell gales it's
Miserable hail; What hope can i distrain?
How do you ask me to canister your domain?

CARE FOR YOU

I think of you everyday
And care for you everyway
We learn along the way
To pave a healthier stay

So what if we live apart
We grow near in heart
I wish to look, listen
And learn from you

I will churn, turn, burn
As i yearn for you
If you're insecure then
I'll be your cure

So there's nothing you can't endure
I really want us to be friends
And to share a love so pure; that
It will be crystal clear, demure!

In my heart you'll always stay
I'll come back to you one sweet day
We'll have love that won't fade away
So you n'me will never be led astray

CARMELITA

Carmelita Has got me singing again
:
        And i am ready to fight
Carmelita Has got me dancing
:   again
        And I'm feeling alright

She's the girl with the awesome
Looks; and she won't give in to
You're sultry, suggestive hooks
You'll fall flat on curvy nooks

There's an aura around the place
She's soft landed from cosmic space
What lovably sweet; divine grace
She slapped me straight in the face

In all the enthralling, wide world
A very special one off angelic girl
Can you swim in the frothing swirl
When she pulls, your pince nez curl

Carmelita Has got me reeling out of sight
:
        Even if my pants are too tight
Carmelita Has got me praying not in vain
:
        Maybe i can cleanse away my pain

CATACOMB SMILE

You're breath oozed pitingly from the
Bruised swollen armpits onto my spine
I sensed uneasiness and radical reform
Flummoxing from a stony catacomb smile

Grappling with the sad tears of life
And the kitschy joys of hype, whilst
Piercing the mists, of shadows black
Persnicketing as your catacomb smile

I don't want to burst, your bubble
Or get you into diabolical trouble
In dead stillness of the cemetery i
Answer the unearthly call then fall

I've slept out in the farsical gutter
That's why i value my bread and butter
Serenity makes you stutter, beckoning
The finality of death and it's clutter

CAUTIOUSLY CRAVE

We learn more from the things
We do wrong than the things
We do right, we acknowledge
The objection and fear rejection

So let's insert, a healthier injection
It's interesting to observe n'subserve
Especially in the slimy twisting curve
I'll be your witty, funny little clown

That will never ever let you down
Everything may seem strange today
Only with care, it's clear as day
You cautiously crave, for love on

The double, wishing to avoid any trouble
I'm not going to do anything dreadful to
You, i just want to share some time with
You; Do you often sense the storm chilly

Weather, when you put two and two together?
The beginning was wrongly connected to the end
Things were moving along much better back then
If you're life is still stuck in the middle

Can you solve the riddle?

CHAMPION

You know it's tough
Out there on the street
And nobody cares if
Your down and beat!

But in your heart you know you
Have to compete; it's compelling
Not to end in defeat: then you
Can have the world at your feet!

Endurance is our energy stamina beat
You must train n'strain every nerve
And muscle fibre in your torso sheet
To possess a solid enviable strength

That's born from sweat and body heat
When the healthy growing pain ripples
Your adrenalin vein, you can blossom
Like a flower with charasmatic power

The desire to be champion
Is more than a mean feat
If you don't excel at what
You do then take a back seat

CHARISMATIC SPELL

Last night seemed a thousand miles away
As we drank, laughed tripped and played
I was happy just to be swayed by you're
Flimsy flippant, funny melodramatic way

I thought i knew you, so pleasantly well
Before you cast you're charismatic spell
I must dive deeper into you're halo well
To decipher what the seer cusps foretell

But love disappointed me rather badly
It made me feel hurt n'negative sadly
So beware of long legged ladies, cute faces
Warm embraces, innocent eyes and lanky lies

CHEEKY CHEEKS

Your cheeky cheeks are so sneaky
They match your spotless smile
That's why i delightfully rile
To run past the four minute mile

When you walk your Jeans do the talk!
Gifted with a sly cat's eye you stalk
So subtle you gawk with mixed emotion
I balk and fly swift like savage hawk

CHUNKY HUNK

I just love your meaty dish, Trish
It's encompassed with hot sauce fish
My stomach hungers wheedling penny
Fishmongers like saturnine wonders

If I'm to act, you'd prefer tact
You require everything slick intact
Though i feel infinitely lost estranged
You comfort me and say love is strange!

Slap me with spunk, show me how you funk
Steer away the skunk; you chunky hunk
Savoir fare with dignified untenable care
Even if we didn't make a fluent start

We've already touched eachother's heart
We cannot afford to drift apart, sublime
Art; i know that I'm not your normal date
But I'm fully grown so we can best relate

CIVIL CIVIC

You've think you've won
But i have not yet begun
To fire lead from zip gun
Flaming bullets filly fry

My posture from tip to toe
Exclamating by lethal foe
Horizontal, vertical blow
Slitting us fast and slow

In a freaky shallow flow
Like a still freakshow
Splitting blow by blow
As a meteor afterglow

With cosmic fallout woe
Aligning the hallowed throw
With supernatural zeal to heal
In a ceremony, what's the deal?

However civil civic our citizens be
How can one remain calm and free?
Plagued by pain n'fee; in a city with
No pity that's camouflaged wicked wity

CIVILIAN STATION

My happy go lucky spirit personifies
Who i am as you're scallywag charm
Pretypifies who you scam, our love
Flips over like the waves crashing on

The white cliffs of Dover, like a double
Headed coin wherever it rolls we'll join
I don't want to loose my concentration
In this frantic cyber civilian station

If we'd exchange some quality time
Would you always like to be mine
I used to really love you at one
Stage but now i just turn the page

You're mind is steamingly powered full of rage
Something must have happened to you long ago
Something that you just don't prefer to show
But now you have a fresh choice, so let it go!

CLEMENT STYLE

A lion kills with nobility n'
Ferocious agility, there's no
Shame or fear even if you can
Disappear, the present tries to

Escape from it's vast endemic past
Peering the dirty crevice downcast
You look so great, dressed in navy
Sand, as i wish to play you like a

Classic baby grand, lend me you're untame
Pedimanous land so I'll eat from your jam
Now it's time to let the genie out of the
Ancient bottle, n'rev up to full throttle

I'm not a private investigator or some
Insurance estimator; you're not an art
Curator or seafaing navigator, don't
Think so contaminated and disanimated

You've become dirigibly distinct, but not
Extinct; be content with life n'disregard
The tripe, your clement style topples the
Gridlock mile, soothing the pensive smile

CLEAN STAIN

What have you come to do?
I've come to cheer up you
If i said I'd give up all
N'everything just for you

Would you think of me true?
Or avoid the sphincter blue
Even when i reached the top
I washed the sop in the mop

I know you'd expect everything
Spick and span but i feel like
An outcast in some sanguinary
Marching regimen; i pray amen

Digesting all which i possibly can
Murmering awkwardly in abating ban
Puddling subterfuge and feruse pan
Floundering a path to halidom clan

Enduring the assailant strappado
With my resourceful prop bravado
Frothing saliva like Lady Godiva
Honey; i don't want to jive you!

Hold you close in picture frame
As i assemble silent pain, your
Clean stain lifts my heavy crane
Systems of pure love, entertain!

CLOSER TO HEAVEN

It's ten to eight as i set
My bait; topsy turvy state
Cuggi shirt, on xmas plate
Hurry for i cannot be late

I'v seen all that i want to see
I'v been all that i want to be
Travelling along i sing a song
And decipher right from wrong

I know it won't be long until i
Prosper from all that's going on
When I'm on the edge I'll make a
Pledge, indignant is the wobbling

Ledge; with our knees hugged to our
Chests, our chins methodically rest
If we pool all of our resources into
Workable forces, we'll be so strong!

We'll have a rehearsal at Rye
And wave bye bye as we eat our
Cherry-pie, we'll soar sky high
Then closer to heaven we'll try

CLOUDS COLLIDE

Why jingle? When you can always mingle
If you push me too far i might as well
Blow up my brand new electric guitar
So go ahead and break my cement head

Pretty soon i shall be more than dead
Haven't you already been properly fed
So why cringe as you show your fringe
Why do you expect me to change my art

How can i part with something that's
Been instilled in my dribbling heart
Your still driving around, on an old empty tank
N'your emotions feel like they temporarily sank

Clouds collide before they disperse n'cry as we run
For shelter to keep us dry, from what? a hidden lie
How selfishly do we try? How can you appoint yourself
Judge n'jury without any evidence just explosive fury

COLLATERAL VIBE

Unusual happenings are occuring for me!
Shall i grasp them before they gasp me?
You hurriedly speak irrational thoughts
From your sourpuss mind; even if unkind

The innocence of your charm bedazzled my yarn
Yqur so mean n'clean, showering off hot steam
I want you first on my team, whose to blame
For your high esteem? Just who do you deem?

Your still a kitten in a mitten; once shy
Twice bitten! Do you grind greasy gears or
Hang some heavy fears? Why somersault pride
With collateral vibe? Must i remember your

Stain of silly vain? Which collided with my
Worn out fain making me think i was lost in
Spain, in the midst of a bullfight, without
A cain! Nevertheless, i can tame your game!

COLLYWOBBLE FROZE

You were so cold to me
That i collywobble froze
Logically i tried to propose
What happened, was mere pose

Your scarf flippant fell
From the crimson tower
Where you were captured by
An evil power, we lay wide

Open to mesmerising pain, as my
Desire ignited in furious flame
Insecurities ran into your mind
Insecurities made you see blind

Your lips tasted like marmalade when i read
And i was your butter spread on fresh bread
You sentenced me to a fate worse than death
Yet i still idolize you with all my breath!

COLONIAL SQUATTER

Colonial squatter on sacred soil
Leave your cabin on the hilltop
And run down into the valley below
Where light dwindles, angels fear to go

Don't put on a cloak to disguise
The hidden fear of mortal eyes
Buffalo skin is hunted downcast
Buzzard's troop the grizzly fast

The bow and arrow were swifter than
The sparrow; the tomahawk left it's
Mark, like raiders of The Holy Ark!
The Winchester shot the savage heart

Blackfoot's ghost still haunts proud
Pagan grounds curdling mighty warrior's
Bones with a craving lust, insatiable
Bust: of once worshipped days of epic

Battles, with blood dripping blades!
Even the jaws of the timber wolf don't
Scar as deep as the memory of that numb
Dreaded day, when the Mohawk tribe fell

Prey. To white man's epidemic of cursed
Hate. Was it justifiable or cruel fate?
This frightful forest possesses myths
Which are no more clearer than mists

Lingering without unravelling a thing
Shrewdly they clutch at you and grin
The protocol of the fox is sabre sly
Even if we use the illuminati eye!

How can we win without incumbent try?
Can we sparkle our submissive high?
Thus the evolving eagle in the sky
Stares down and wonder's why

Human history goes on and on
Nothing has changed for a change
It's just the same, just the same
Isn't that a wondering shame?

COMMON CONSTITUTION

When the farmers who work
High up, in the mountains
Come down to our tiny town
They feel glad mighty glad

Yet, they put on a show
To dissemble their disgust
Because they haven't found trust
The words that they speak are of

Great wealth and riches with stealth
Protruding knowledge is genuine health
Reserved to only a few, credit is due!
How totally unexpected, is fate's cue?

In life there's always a crunch
Even with the most sincere bunch
A tainted hunch: sample the poison
At the next thanksgiving lunch!

Twentieth century novelty has now
Relinquished most of our heritage
No matter how complex and efficient
Modern machines may be; they cannot

Replace the parish priest, for he is a
Holy solution to our common constitution
Of many wicked institution, sphered evil
Like high voltage elocution in evolution

COMPETITION IS EVERYWHERE

Competition moves everywhere!
Making me aware of everything
That's precious to me to wear
It pops straight up and barks

Leaving it's mark in miserable dark
Sailing in a tossing raft like Noah's
Ark; it makes me perform super sonic
Even though I'm not a stand up comic

I just work sub sonic and inject my
Business tonic, my blood pressure is
Nearing chronic so platonic! it feels
Superior, mocking your pious interior

Weaving love lest yarns, through it's
Oyster charms; Do you have any qualms?
Do you receive enough attentive palms?
On the competitive rail parallel trail

How do you confront the cul de sac tail?
When your furious cross who do you toss?
Do you crack up or try to comfort the loss?
Shall you compete with your alter-ego boss?

COMPLIANT EYE

In the enchanting mould some harmony tolled
My chariot raced thru a procession of solid
Motorcade; into swifter shades of trade far
Away in country lade filled chaparral spade

The beefy cattle stomps; with a hefty rattle
My ailing mind aloofs my virgin heart spoofs
I lay fidgeting in the dust and marking time
Sombering without a compliant eye as i await

For the siesta to begin, now i wish to dine
I seek bubbles of wine, from the fresh vine
Caviar and oysters, champagne served on time
cuban cigars, n'soft playing spanish guitars

COULDN'T BE UNFAITHFUL

You're everything and more than i could ever
Ask for, you heal my every little virus sore
You're the only one that i virtuously live for
With each passing day, I'll yearn for you more

I will pay the top price as i purchase the
Roulette dice n'try to win the·merchandise
That'll be so sweet and nice, as i eagerly
Rove with my platonic chaperoned blue eyes

Flaringly tosticating somewhere above the skies
I couldn't be unfaithful to you even if i tried
I could never ever look at you honestly straight
In you're innocent cute tender maiden face n'lie

COUNCIL CIVIC

I like the way you wear your hair
But i really do need intensive care
I'm not a fancy new age tailor or
An adventurous swashbuckling sailor

I just like to taste the ice cream flavour
You must have been a princess in a past life
As i secretly made love to you and wanted you
As my wife, nowadays i have to avoid the strife

We have to keep all the nasty omens away
Whilst sifting through the leisurely hay
Running desperately out, from harm's way
Replacing the tragic with something magic

Money has to be counted to be very specific
Does all the evidence have to be scientific
Love horrific, prophets prolific, status terrific
Mundane lives are always stalked by council civic

CUPID'S ARROW

Cupid's arrow hissed, it's romantic sound
On it's lovable aphrodisic courting round
Encarnalising hearts, to a phonetic pound
I wish i could grab it's shiny lovely bow

I would sparkle brightly from head to toe
I could untangle this messy entrechat foe
Then you n'me will satedly sensually relax
Like every other adoring couple to the max

What character trait do you set as bait
Contesting such a lovely fortunate fate
The art of love is mesmermsingly inspiring
Your hand in marriage is what I'm desiring

CUTE MUTE

Don't peep at me strange!
I'm not deranged just short changed
Don't make me walk the pirate's plank
I might spill into a dead end prank

She's five foot six n'gets her kicks
When she only just turned twenty-one
She bought a double barrel shotgun
And shot the pants off Bullseye-Won!

Her eyes contrite the deepest stare
Flushing decisive immaculate hair
She's so cute, she can't be mute!
You encompass my hook so don't sook

Why feed me to the inimical sharks?
I'v just stepped out of gimical parks
When you stammer smile imeditate for a
While then i store my file in your pile

Collaborating on the elite mega mile
I must acquaint myself in bisque style
And shake off the unpleasant risque vile
To arabesque my love for more than a while

CYNICISM'S CUP

You're always on cue and never blue
You have a right to acquire n'fire
Can you possibly climb much higher
It's only you that i totally desire

The wind waves your straggly bleached
Blonde hair without the slighest care
The light bulb flitted, as you impatiently
Slitted your dress down the dimly lit lane

I've dreamt of a thousand different dreams
Perpetuated with hideous fears and screams
You're ego needs a placebo instead of a gazebo
It's no use running on a battery flat, or even

Straddling upon a dirty dusty slippery mat
I'm not a psychologist or an archaeologist
It's the hidden things, which i search n'seek
Why drink from cynicism's cup when it's bleak

DEATH

As your treading in the danger zone
Death greets you with a deadly tone
You feel like an air filled balloon
You can't escape it's hounding pace

Which delivers the final resting place
It won't ask anyone what have you done
To be spared my solitary grimmacing hum
Which is expelled from my automatic gun

Death cheats not even an innocent soul
It guarantees a heartless restful cold
Clutching it's victims annihilatingly bold
Mesmerising then pulling you in by the arm

Capitulating with a distinct harmful charm
Once in the doors lock as your life docks
The maps are useless, there's no way out
We cannot summon, the orthodox sprout!

DECADENT HASTE MAKES WASTE

Jordan has a madman on his mind
That spins in a whirlwind just fine
There's nothing more to mention till he goes
He's so understanding that he knows

To separate nonsense from the pro's
Winners lose and losers win
How can you tell it is so?
It's a paradox, don't you know?

The bending spoon stirs but does not grow
It's an optical illusion to some conclusion
A ticklish rhetoric, all ready to go like
A circus show; Angry rivers reveal their

Paste, decadent haste makes them waste
The truthful colours of their tender youth
Pollution stacks up too, so what can they do?
It's now all up to me and you!

DEEP NESCIENCE

You have to be beaten, as to understand
How to beat then you can achieve a much
Higher feat n'relish in it's valuable treat
When you sit upon the bosses seat, you look

Quite neat, lisping words of solitude and
Deep nescience, you don't intend to emerit
You're public position which has brought you
So much recognition fuelled by kaotic ambition

Do you secretly crave, such a thrilling supposition
Whilst wearing a sunaroid i quickly captured you on
Polaroid, you're empattement was gutted negatively void
As my creative mind reclined to read a fabled palidrome

Like arid stubble dusty plains, blended with bare brains
Sinuating with aching love alternating the chamois glove
I'm no seer; but i can slide away you're falling tear
And comfortably lift you up to my crater stratosphere

Everyone knows that I'm a despot on a sour glory trot
It's Pegasus that *i* ride, upon the great southern sky
Every conflicting puzzle needs a happy wealthy muzzle
Life spills like sinuous rills! Can it offer thrills?

DEMOTING OUR STRIPE

Why did you leave me that night?
Standing alone without any hype!
Twas a case of demoting our stripe
I resorted to smoking a bigger pipe

Filling the statuesque tray with ash
While fondling my sleight petty cash
Which i slotted then safely stashed
Rumours soon surfaced of how i knew

That your behaviour was split in two
The supple psyche; indentured in you
Eccentrically i screamed, to let off steam
But no one seemed to be on my winning team

By moonlight my foot grew light, then i had
A terrible fight, with my face shut so tight
I belted at the lucid chiming, marble night
Even that didn't resolve my inhibiting fright

DEPTH OF MISERY

You never waited for me
You only wanted to be free
Always running here n'there
Could not stay could not care

For anybody but yourself
Never lied about your past
Ev n though it did not last
The things you craved for so

Desperately, did not eventuate
For you to be, look back at your
Perplexing coffin tree; slithering
Worms parasite hack in you and me!

I'm begging to escape this intensity
N'the scathing avalanche of monstrosity
Life's reflecting anxiously, it's sweet
Depth of misery; fortune scars lie bare

Recklessly they drive you to nowhere
Insanity is a huge meagre biting pain
Please deliver this evil from my brain
Unleash the infected vile from our vein

DESIDERATUM NICHES

I noticed the chill of shock wending it's
Way behind your verdant vale intoning the
Genuflections of intermontane viaducts in
Seasoned vernacular, with virulent chants

We'll have picnics, in the cool surfing breeze
And shower underneath the fresh steamy cascade
We'll rove up and down the moist green gullies
N'white sandy coral beaches desirously running

Alongside the dessicate tidal inlet creatures
There are no despicable reprobate features in
Our chattels of wealth, swathing favourably to
Aspersing the dulcet of the desideratum niches

DESTINY ISN'T VANITY

After ransacking my entire personal fortune
You converge n'splurge in a wave of frantic
Excitement! What future strategy conceals
The paragon of excess that you've amassed

For less? Those days cross over much faster
When there is an aptitude; for grand master
Destiny isn't vanity, nor insanity! How can
You stay on the ball when it's easy to fall

Did you properly digest and re set all you're
Pithily financial gears? Is you're profession
An obsession or some signed sealed confession
Let's hope it's not another gushing recession

It must be such a thrill, to chalk up the bill
And then run prudently and quickly to the till
We shant get off at the usual penthouse floor
I just need to find an evolving specimen door

DISMISSING UNCERTAINTY

There are much greater treasures than silver n'gold
My battleship scars keep tigwelding my bones of old
The cumulative participants share harebrained schemes
Emanating from unearthly voyages n'pirate ship dreams

There's a dismissing uncertainty in my suppressed psyche
Harnessing the force and furnacing the fire from my wife
Can your love guide me thru rrials n'tribulations of srrife
Thumbscrewing the ailments n'diseases from my tortured life

DO I STILL FIGURE IN YOUR EYE?

Every time we meet
We make out we're discreet
Do we have to hide love away?
Must we be obsessed with play?

Do i still figure in your eye
Do you still jolt foolish pride
I was the guy you used up dry
Why don't you cuddle my hair

Why don't you tickle me bare
I try to hide still swollen tears
Which i muted with blushing fears
As i drink my mind awkward blinks

Don't be content by just having
A flick with any prick, remember
To make it stick! Do i still figure
In your eye? If not, I'll just die!

DO YOU HEAR THOSE ANGELS CALLING?

Do you hear those angels calling?
Do you see they're love, gently falling
A warm apposition in light spring
Flying off to mountains like petal wing

An optimistic feeling, they can conquer all
Of the darkness that surrounds our thoughts
In this world, to fasten the grin on our king
Wrapped up in a social merriment of xmas sing

Do you hear those angels calling?
Do you see they're love, gently falling
Taking us up higher, in a virgin cloud of
Godly tenderness to meet our saviour king

DON'T LEAVE HATE TO MATE

Your my flower in and out of sunshower
I gently watch you passing every hour
Together we'll yield a stronger power
Illuminating from love tower; not sour

You obfuscate the obiter dictum file
In future press dial for no ugly smile
The pure pile lays in style hungry eyes
Spit delicious delightful alibi's; rise

The birth of the blues made trumpeting
Musical rave reviews, from the cotton
Fields and our mammy's yarns grew the
Legacy of black man's slavery charms!

Purple pain rained, piercing my vein
It cued feud but i still sow tow
In crumbling bow i still call no
To bandage bondage; blister sister

Deep south sister, confederate eruption
Organised corruption brought disruption
After defeating glove; grew Yankee love
Fly high butterfly from the gust cocoon

To gas balloon, try pry otiose cry
Fungus tongue in dead domain hung
Hurdle curdle from eccentric girdle
Squelch belch Irish, Scottish, Welch

Lavish ravish, optimum savage
Have·no pity for shifty nifty
Let mind mellow silver yellow
Don't leave hate to mate; fellow!

DRY WINTER

In dry winter, i rescued you
You were bored had little to do
Running about without any clout or clue
I solely trusted you, but then you flew

Dead leaves danced as the wind blew them by
They tumbled from green, to bitter dry
Even the black widow kissed my cheek
As we dozed off, to fast asleep

One dark morning i heard you say
You did not want me to stay
I quickly ran to my car
But my shoe got stuck in the tar

I felt embarrassed n'wept slightly blue
I had a chill all over you
Your love was so very dry
It even caused my garden to die

You were so confused you just
Did not know, what to do
In dry winter, i rescued you
You were bored had little to do

EAGER TO THRILL

I dream of kissing your freshly painted
Purple venom lips, and gently unzipping
Your paper thin satin armani mini skirt
Then squeezing your sultry slender body

Towards mine; amidst the cool night air
I know that your eager to thrill, and i
Won't instill a chill instead I'll drink
The latest high potency aphrodisiac pill

I remember how gorgeously sexy you look
In you're pink body hugging latex dress
With matching shining stiletto's you're
So delectably scrumptious, i must bless

The ambient waving of you're silky long dark
Hair briskly massaging my face sends shivers
Kaleidoscoping up and down my spine, you're so
Sensually tempting i can't rest till your mine

EAT AWAY MY BRAIN

I thought i had everything
Till i met you, then i
Realised how utterly empty
N'untrue, feeling blue

I wish to wipe the mud
From your face that's
Taunting such disgrace
I am under your spell

So why put me thru Hell
Don't eat away my brain
Just munch out my pain
I don't need you just

To like me for what i do
I want you to like me
Only, and no one new
So How do you do?

Won't you explore my point
Please re-occupy my joint
If you want me let me know
If not, quickly let me go

ELEVATE YOURSELF

Your a product of the Wall Street collapse
And the reserve credit squeeze slash
If there's another stock market crash
You might lose your money in a flash

You despise all forms of tax
Which erode your profit to the max
Your a high roller ensnaring the garrison axe
I'm going to sign a petition to carve out the

Competition; What manoeuvre will secure us Denver Hoover?
Your edification is like the mint, tip top in every stint
With too many colours rolled into one you've got to look
Out for number one, especially in business then for fun!

Don't duck shuffle the interest rate kerfuffle
Happy is a heart that give; the halo bigger lives
Do you want a million dollar deal or an accredited
Government guaranteed seal? What a jaw dropping "till

Can you recite the law of tort or seek to be held
In contempt of court? Do you embezzle the portfolio
Management trust or liquidate the company's annuity
Superannuation scheme, for your greedy little lust?

As you climb the corporate ladder your bank account
Grows much fatter, your assets are pristine matter!
Your hideaway cottage is been sprayed with a newage
Solvent anti-rust; now it's been classified by the

National Trust, the bogus offing is hindsight
Topping, you won't inherit a bird bath flopping
Like an oil baron tycoon your shares will zoom
The stock exchange can leave you short of change

Multi-level-marketing is the alacrity, residual income
Game: I'm sick of ingenious armchair backroom politicians
And crafty, backstabbing, slanting, intellectual, mordant
Technicians, when this is over I'll sail the cliffs of Dover

Maybe we can sip ice tea on the isle of Capri
And drink pina colada by the sparkling sea
You can't devulge a wretched bankrupt subconscious
Instead you've got to elevate yourself with clear conscious

ELUSIVE

Something beautiful something worthwhile
One thing wonderful jumped in style
I cherished it with all my heart
Because it made me super smart

As it brought me much unfounded leisure
Which really devulged truest pleasure
That was my vault to supreme treasure
Giving it rings n'tons of things

For many seasons i worshipped the
Elusive thing respecting it like
King and Queen; being fancy free
Did not suffice the need in me

I felt bitterly blue when old
Elusive left no clue: So what
Could i do? Those days are now
Long gone, only memory calls on

EMOTIONS RISE

Your youthful chant haunts my tender soul
Extracting my ambition fold resisting any
Thing of old, recklessly i try but can't
Escape it's realm, mystery n'imagination

Surrounds it's helm, surfacing twist n'elm
Today i laughed at life and it giggled at me
As a ferris-wheel rotates it's passengers weary
Ego transcending vibes send tides to my thighs

Shattering mirrors reflections of self
By hurling rocks into a passive lake
Snorting ripples make plankton awake
Wonder at the magic at nature's gate

Aching to mind whiffing in skin, hacking
At my jaws it wheezes chin; socket slim?
Making sure it's a once off limb anxious
To check every bolt n'rim: Emotions rise

As do the tides of the mighty immortal sea
Replenishing the earth with it's notoriety
Solitude softly sways the enormous fins of
The Great Blue whale with it's Moby Dick tail

Hard-nosed, massive is it's gale, knowing
When to sing it's song capsising sailor's
Forever long, even the king of the sea has
Misery, premium is the price for serenity!

EVEN WITH TEAR I'LL PERSERVERE

Even with tear I'll persevere
And wipe away your inner fear
I'll shift swiftly to top gear
And peak the horizon's sphere!

Like the mythical unicorn, clear
I'm at the crossroads of my life
So now i must keep out of strife
I'll ponder at my past n'present

Life so i can fire-up like some
Sharp shooter on my motorcycle
Scooter, with my repertoire of
Faith, our requiem is all safe!

EVERYONE REGRETS SOMETHING

It's a sign of desperation as
You say, you want to flex the
Upperhand, i can't understand
Why you're not in a very nice

Relationship, to love and be loved
My brain feels like a plane that's
Just runway landed skidding on the
Wet tarmac n'left solely abandoned

Your dimure chest expands, like words
Slandered; everyone regrets something
But not everything, i cannot stand to
Loose you again, i just wish to dream

Of you and me sharing a much deserved
Tropical island holiday, you know how
I love cake giving, as much as you adore
Flower receiving so let's stop deceiving

EXCALIBUR

Magic sword of unfathomed vows, curt
And bury dragons mouths, whoever pulls
It free, shall be the rightful king for
All of England to see; so be the prophecy

Power and wisdom will be granted like a key
As Arthur decrees the right to royal throne
After he fiercely pulls the sword from stone
Camelot city built by fairy kings and queens

To the sound of angelic music, castle supreme
Spires n'turrets focus serene; at the tourney
Prizes weren't more than a lady's glove or veil, but
Everyone was pleased to kneel, sovereign was the feel

Dying with honour was a valiant thrill! In High Hall
Arched knights deemed and schemed their blessed march
To serve king and country was their exalting parch
Revealing mystic visions and appanage apparitions

On the tourney ground they made apotheosis stance
And fought eachother with ferocity sword and lance
Chivalrous rules they must endow for their faith is
Christendom, however proficient at weaponary be remain

Kind to vassals n'henchmen plea; "My coat of arms can
Proudly exhibit me". A hundred n'fifty knights vowed
Themselves to the quest, remembering it's a fanciful
Turbulent test: but the Holy Grail only appears to

Those who have reached pure perfection in spirit vest
It is prophesised, don't you know? That a knight. born
On May Day will forward come to split the Brotherhood
Of Camelot from united won! Mordred, who is this one?

Merlin, is it really out off enchanting hand?
To try to change this cursed evil crooked stand!
Will Excalibur prevail, victorious or flutter pale?
Lady of the Lake can you feed us a magic porridge cake?

We'll need supernatural strength to slay the cunning
Serpent snake; Arthur, it's time to vacate this earth
And saintly re-birth, into the heroic kingdom of noble
Immortal worth, ascending to the unanimous democratic

Round table, with it's heavenly awing gable and it's
Knights of christian fable; Arthur will be escorted to
Avalon as a royal guest, to offset the enemy pest and to
Halidom rest until England summons his never ending quest!

EXOTIC LOTION

I don't want emotion lacking devotion
It's like a barren desert for erosion
With sullen distinct bomber promotion
Fervid culling was my perpetual ocean

Which triggered undue minor explosion
Ha:r;rowing became your major commotion
Tw ngling a sense of the exotic lotion
Transpiring relativity a loving potion

EXRUCIATE BUNDLE

After you jump in the well
You can go to bloody Hell!
That's how i bleeding feel
Over your awful ruddy smell

Honest people have the right
To lead healthy honest life
With plenty of vigour; ripe
No elusive mutter nor snipe

You arbitrate distraction
Through aggregate faction
Why inadequate satisfaction
To reduce unpleasant action

Give straight-forward jargon
Exalting argon within pardon
How can your serenade be humble
When you can excruciate bundle?

FAITH IN LIFE

Climb that mountain to the top
When you reach it you will see
All there is to feel; and more
When you climb the big mountain
You can drink from the fountain

Have faith in yourself, in your friends
Faith in every single thing that you do
With faith in life, all things are nice
You shall see and feel a brighter world
So share you're faith, around the world

FAME HAS MOVED YOU TO A HIGHER FLOOR

Arguments are exchange of ideas
That are firmly held dear
We shouldn't be afraid
If we've nothing to fear

I got castigated in my own
Spider web and weighed in like a
Blockhead; my eyes reflected red
As you weaved debilitating thread

Where are your forces?
Have they left their sources?
Your problem needs detention
Better still, prevention; which

Is not a new invention: languidly
Do you debate, rebate, or oscitate?
Submissively you've been indocrinated
To think; your a jack-in-the-box which

No one can criss-cross or ferry toss
You used to be sagacious
So why change to fallacious?
I liked you better before

You were sad and poor
Now your rich but sore
Status has changed your door
Fame has moved you to a higher floor

FASTIDIOUS INSIDIOUS

My mind jolts to ascend
As you vent your descend
From fast fading flowers
Scraped away in dusty towers

Menaced by hungry hours;
I know your a complex girl
Wrapped up in a vivid world
Your a hot for hire call

Dining at a high class ball
You yield your shield
To first class appeal
You can't be a cheap flirt!

That's why i wear expensive shirt
To pitter patter, petty petulance
Fastidious insidious i alien lay
As you break, my sturdy foreplay

FATE FROM SPELL

Your searching for a new love
Cause the old one was peeling
Your looking for a new feeling
Cause the old one was kneeling

Many people find it hard to forgive if
They assume negatively, suspiciously
Unforgivingly unto others, therefore
They sail the critical shore, omitting

Paradise raw; friend or foe I'll bake
The dough, fried or roasted I'll keep
You posted there's always another rhyme
To fill a new line; sunshine, somehow i

Don't think it's meant to be for you to
Get together with me so let's not fling
Onto the same tree shaking as it may be
Faking a storm breaking, don't be prone

To take blood from stone; you will succumb to
My clever clone aesthetic dome: wearing pendant
Unknown, only time will tell if I'v done so well
Can i distinguish fate from spell n'purify Hell?

FAULT OF FICTION

I was looking for me
You were looking for you
We both got caught up in two
I'm crazy about you in every way

To get you I'll use any cliche
So what more do i have to say
To steal your heart and run away
Everyone has a crinkle, so it's simple

Thru torrid marshes, soot and muck always
Remember to safely duck then unpluck, even
If your out of luck; the ceiling is pealing
Very badly, my heart is feeling pretty sadly

Is it fault of fiction that leaves us with
An endless addiction to a new prescription
Like a chant from primeval times, our lives
Spin hastily in a rare kaleidoscope of hope

Focusing on the atmospheric poke, amoeba scope
That's no joke, with just a swift single stroke
Constricting upon us it's deadly choke, can you cope
To be left all alone, depraved crippled and disowned

FINGERLICK MY BATTERED PRIDE

I had a notion of perpetual motion
N'lasting devotion of love emotion
Come take me across the spiral sky
And fingerlick my battered pride!

It's hard to tell
Who's lost and won
When no one smiles
It's just not fun

What am i looking for?
Is it on the step of my front door?
Statues don't talk but we can hear them
They cannot move; yet we fear them!

The mantle piece doesn't rest in peace
Like fallen comrades; now deceased!
There has to be a method in your madness to
Eradicate the sadness n'bring forth gladness

Don't dig yourself into a hole like a stupid
Frenzied mole; take time to relax the foul
Fin-de-siecle, is the analogy future role
To a perverse anathema of astringent soul

Is your life really worth the war?
What are you still fighting for?
If you can't do good then don't do bad
Because I'v seen everything that's sick n'sad

FIRST INCEPTIONS

All my first inceptions
Were full of deceptions
Venting bad receptions
Intended as acceptions

From higher exemptions
With small preventions
To all my intentions
Just not contentions

But by exasperations
Of cheap flirtations
All my first inceptions
Were full of deceptions

FLEDGELING STRAIN

Everyone needs action for personal
Satisfaction sentiments are devised
By the pertinent one who sideswipes
The sun, conducting deliberate fun

Psyche twisted beyond ozone haze
Whilst heart fringed inside maze
Your face lacked not meagre pace
Floundering snitching tedium ace

Your adoring eyes don't drift apart
Then i calmly know your super smart
Whisper in my ear if you don't want
Anyone else to hear or come so near

Don't patter in accosting vain or
Wrestle with the ice cooling rain
Abstain from life's mediocre train
Shelter yourself from fledgeling strain

FLOODING FACE

I cannot forget you even if i tried
You're a whole part of me n'my life
I will love you till the day i die
You can't sense exactly how i feel

You're strutted love sounds like a dying dog
Barking lonely in the dry brown leafy gutter
Hardened by useless idle moribundled flutter
Randomly tumbling inside an overflowing bowl

I'll watch out for you're unsymmetrical cold
You're russet flooding face is extremely out
Of place; burnished stoicly in sloppy disgrace
My heart spins pitifully like a worn out wheel

Trying to cash in big on the elusive roulette deal
Tightening my belt buckle, as i hear you're throat
Chuckle n'you're face ruckle, I've become sharper now
Than before because you've opened up your closed door

FLUORESCENT FRIGHT

The sun flashes it's prominence, dictating
It's dominance blustering opalescent ominous
Throughout our solar system it enhances very
Persistant there's a stratum quite consistant

Like the monotonous beat of the drum snare
It battles the elements blare profusely it
Hovers like a hare, issuing it's decorum
Proverbial share of cosmic tide and care

Our hearts are beating while we're meeting
My purse is eating, the snow is bleating
Sorry for only fleeting my viable greeting
Why do you put me in the dirt with quirt?

Never a line out to acute stout, under a
Pretext of freshness clever words fluctuate
Enigma bright, sheer charisma excluding trite
Which store is cuffing light fluorescent fright?

FOOLING THE FOOL

Everyone needs to need
Everyone wants to want
We can pick and choose
Even if we tend to lose

We don't heed the abuse
Of being used n'disused
We all can cover enough
To hide our stuffy duff

All these girls that think they can fool
All those guys who think they're so cool
Where are they now? Do you see them at all?
Are they still cool? Or fooling the fool?

So don't despair my sweet innocent lovely
As you walk down those cold empty streets
My heart lays down right there with you
My bowl is yours, however pallid to eat

When you tuck yourself in your bed
You can think of me and gently tred
And when you hear the early bird call
You can dream in your sleep, is that all?

All these girls that think they can fool
All those guys who think they're so cool
Where are they now? Do you see them at all?
Are they still cool? Or fooling the fool?

FOREVER TRUE

Baby tonight we're going back
In time, to when we first met
It clicked and chimed; tonight
I'm going to take you back and

Make you remember how things
Used to be in my sweet amber
You made me pander, as i yelled
Out deceit slander: petty anger

Baby tonight, I'm going to ignite
My proscenium flame altruistically
Secure your main aim depriving you
Of charnel domain, maximizing gain

You glisten my fickle, tender sickle
Can you resist the tempting trickle?
A woman like you makes me feel very
Complete, the others i just delete!

Ambidextrous n'gallant we'll hang on too
In a hullabaloo I'll cork your screw
I'll even plumb my way to Timbuktu
For you, I'll remain forever true!

FORMIDABLE DECISION

I really respect what you are
And what you do, when i see you
Walk down the aisle my sad heart
Jumps up with an embracing smile

I heavenly rile my unique satin style
Upmost is my denial to degenerate vile
Updating your conversant file i know how
Explicably picturesque you solemn dream

To imagine a world of peace and right
Without darkness to distract the light
Just amplify auspicious white with the
Humble dawning of the unanimous right

Within us their's a formidable decision
Of ingratiating attaining mission, let's
Revitalize revision; omitting indecision
Crystallizing vision to new world precision

FRANTIC ROMANTIC

When i alight from the fast train
Don't bother to leave your filth
That stains, if it means leaving you
For someone else then i must make up

My mind and choose for greater wealth
I'm no dill to intake drug n'pill for
My thrill; i need to watch the bill!
Though i middy clown in agonism antic

I'm a slapstick rebel, frantic romantic
Behind the bedroom curtain you patiently
Tell me to wait till we wed, honey let me
Remind you at this turtle rate we'll never

Make it to bed! What happened to the slap
And tickle that we read? Huff n'puff like
Wonderstuff, your a flagellant dragon whose
Just swallowed a red flagon: you slap brisk

Cuddle n'kiss, wow, what bliss! I cannot miss!
I swear with might that I'm only right so stop
The fight and serenade plenty of pleasure with
Delightful leisure, i don't intend to be brash

But i just have to flash my scabby jagged rash
Headstrong lash, slavish cash, dissident trash
Neath the wreckage stash, there's a heart to heart
Call, saying love should be a ball even if we fall

FRENZIED ANGST

There are so many hurdles, to trample over
Before you can win the gruelling long race
At such a demonstrably fast dangerous pace
Colluding in self brutallisation and a tad

Of mental humiliation, scuppered in some
Frenzied angst, chortingly spritzing the
Soporific embodiment ostracised out of
Edifice manoeuvres, now is the time to

Tackle your grind, then chain whip your
Pride into the glitziest ferocity still
Simmering overblown in a sculling drone
Ticklish evil is it's tone; in a throne

Light years away from any domestic home
Iconic accoutrements are pirouetting so
Scantly clad? Untested with some excess
Baggage of a steadfast, miffing routine

FRIGID SOUL

Spider spider on the wall be careful
Not to fall, into a bowl of porridge
Scolding hot, too hot; then fly can not
Roam in the air n'zip around everywhere

Steer clear from the pressure pack lair
Be aware to land safely below down there
Don't let heavy chains bind your stalking walk
Shake off your dusty chalk as you blarney talk

Don't be distressed by maiden's vows
Navigate a free course forever proud
If not enchanted anyhow, there lies
A crypt of cobra vipers for you now

Slight and short compile to naught; abort!
Born too soon, gone for noon, what a tune?
Death greets it's victims with rigid coal
It feels the need to win, new frigid soul

Like you read a dead sea scroll, as written
By the seers of Atlantis it subtely appears
And puzzles scholarly peers, like antique
Vanished treasures in sunken seabed years

Cruising the abyss atlas is the epitome
To coercively foresee destiny
Be weary of travels and ails
Thankful only ..... to where you avail!

FRUSTRATION BIT YOU SORE

That was the last straw
You couldn't take it anymore
Frustration bit you sore
Striking your inner pore

I know that you did care
So why not still be fair?
When i put on a zany show
Man do i go; eclectic i row

Rueful is my untamed neolithic foe
Everything went sour in the past hour
Yet we subdued the seep midnight power
I don't want to be a secondhand retreat

Or a roving satellite, wacked off-beat
I wish to orbit your daily planet beat
You tried to find true love but you only
Faked it, when you had the chance you

Should of raked it! Tell me true.
How Sweet are you? I can try to understand
Why you deceived me with sleight of hand
However, I'm proud to still withstand

GANGSTER

What's this web of intrigue and conspiracy
To deceive? My company pays top dollar for
Me to keep it's honour!. How can you be a
Bleak impostor when you snoop to foster?

Do you need a lobotomy for your dog-eat-dog
Posture?. Have you hid the laundered black
Money in your .38 calibre shoulder holster?
Whizzing with your stand over tactic poster

Don't dangle with ephemeral lustre
Or try to be a ghost-buster muster
All your tough men from waterfront
Bars that smoke huge cigars abrupt

Is the gangster's job, if you don't
Like it; then shut your bloody gob!
Someone has got to do the dirty work
In this crime ridden underworld town

Especially when the cops aren't around
Don't molest or harass the underground
It suppresses the beefy low life sound
And doesn't arrest it's punters pound!

Many pillars of society are on the take
Be careful i might put a bomb in your cake
If I'm double crossed I'll expose the fake
There's more than meets the eye at stake!

Blackmail and extortion are part of my trait
If I'm expendable, your surrendable as bait
The dapper don and the ex-con exchange vows
And ungodly powers they co-ordinate a cohort

That works mainly after hours, comforting the
Seedy flowers; drug trafficking n'prostitution
In business towers, my mind often cow rs as to
The extent of our cad organised mobster powers

I'm not a prankster just a worn out gangster
My foes keep me on my toes; tommy-gun woes
My fee stings like a bee: in this business
I issue violence and keep my code of silence

GENTLY SUCCUMB

Have you ever seen an eagle fly
Without wings or a dolphin swim
Without fins? Why don't you believe
Me when i say that *i* truly like you

Is it that someone else has rudely
Hurt you before with the same line
Then didn't even knock on your sad
Back door, so why suffer some more

I'll endeavour to comfort you're
Lonely bitter stare and take you
Higher, with comical loving care
I know I'm not the sharpest nail

In the draw but i can huddle you on
The floor, you're a lady of worldly
Charm; would you gently succumb and
Fall, for my innocent, sweet yarn?

GHETTOES FROM BLACK TURN TO WHITE

You dance under a hypnotic trance
But can you understand the magic of your dream?
For the world is frozen with symbols
As it stands, there is no imagery within imagery

Stranded souls have no place to rest
Waiting for the universal light
Ghettoes from black turn to white
When the unearthly being creeping calls

There won't be anytime to congenially rejoice
The harmonic splendour of earth's flavour
Can i sip enchanting nectar from your fruit?
Is it too late for repentance or prayer?

Mother's amuse themselves with plastic games
Children cling to their father's aims
Not knowing what futures lie in time
How can society withstand this crime?

Of underdog suffering, heavy handed cluttering
Internal bleeding; smutty robust hate
There has to be a better way
To live on earth without decay!

GOLDEN MEAN

Aristophanes, Sophocles wrote good natured
Plays: tragic, ridiculing superstitious
Custom ways; Eureka! Archimedes engineered
The Archimedean screw, a majestic marvel

Adding buoyancy to amphibian crew
He forefathered the laser beam too!
In geometry Euclid's work was new
The Elements n'axioms move through

Hipparchus mapped the stars for me n'you
Medicine; what else is eclectic brew?
The Hippocratic Oath is right on cue
An ethic obliged by graduates few

Alexander collected the first zoo
And spread civilization wherever new
Alas! what else is there left to do?
For a race so small but tip-top true

Democritus introduced the atomic theory
Pythagoras deduced the numeric query
If your feeling down, not able, don't
Worry, there's always an Aesop's iable

Isocrates the rhetoric orator was a shy
Public narrator who starved himself later
Anaximander refuted propaganda; the origin
Of life evolved from primitive salamander!

Horner's epic poem, play, has inspired
Poet writer through generation's clay
Sappho's love lyric was often satiric
Rhyming specific in nature prolific

Pindar's choral mode was triumphal ode
Narrating religious moral tithe n'tone
Herodotus recorded history's page citing
Myths and legends of Greece's Golden Age

"Man is the measure of all things"
Is a maxim stated by Pratagoras
"The world is in a state of flux"
Is a doctrine echoed by Heraclitus

Moderation and Temperance
Are virtues of the Golden mean
Fostered in Ancient Greece's dream
A central path for all to follow serene

Debating politics Pericles brought reform
To the Athenian norm issuing pension form
He went ahead with the temple Parthenon
It's marble columns elegantly withstood

Centuries of war and ultra-violet ray
A monumental antique; virgin nay
A chapel of worship and purity prey
Our WORLD WONDERS must be preserved A

GRAVEL

Gravel gravel my mind is spinning
Like gravel
Gravel gravel my mind is spinning
Like gravel

She'd play flirting games of hard
To get, thus tormenting my heart
She'd run to me then to you what a
Flaming tart deceiving my fine art

If she knew how i wanted her
She would beg me to stay
If she knew what I'd do for her
She would always lay

Gravel gravel my mind is spinning
Like gravel
Gravel gravel my mind is spinning
Like gravel

Now I'm lost then I'm found
Squirting every inch n'pound
Barking like a backyard hound
Rolling in a junkyard mound

Nevertheless my caring heart
Wants to soothe her restless mind
Nevertheless i try to remind
My love for her is for all time

Gravel gravel my mind is spinning
Like gravel
Gravel gravel my mind is spinning
Like gravel

What sort of a state am i in
I'm drumming like Micky Finn
Please forgive my grin, don't throw
Me in the bin just take me to my kin

She still offers me succulent kisses
Irresistable **hisses; it never misses**
Bittersweet **divine,** I'm suckling to
Love unkind, bleeding soul and mind

Gravel gravel my mind is spinning
Like gravel
Gravel gravel my mind is spinning
Like gravel

GREEK AS CAN BE!

I'm as Greek as can be
And i buzz like a bee
I'm so shifty you can't see
That i climb Mt. Olympus tree

      At the glendi, I'm trendy levendi
      Afendi, as i drink my ouzo, i drown
      Into a clown n'frizzy frown, i yell n'
      Hound, at all the pretty ladies around

I don't mind their mediterranean mind
I just want to sip their erotic wine
Especially when I'm on top i crop and pop!
It's melodrama, cosmorama, audience shock!

      When I'm out i rage i even make front page
      I command centre stage; Open up the cage!
      Well, I'm just a Greek freak that's why i
      Toot beep! beep! in my beat-up Monaro heap

I can't afford a brand new Mercedes cheap
If the roadrunner raced me he'd be obsolete
Because I'm Greece lightning on my feet!
Donkey's bray as i blimey sway, in sunny

Siesta, the shepherd's flock runneth away
The Parthenon still stands even today
Hellenic beauty has blessed our stay
Democratic culture has paved our way

Philosophy and freedom has shown
The world a better day!•. Logic;
What more is there to say? Plato
Aristotle, reason: come what may

The Olympic flame is a universal parade
When athelete's compete in sports, play
Democracy is the solution to the world's
Bureaucratic, procrastic, array; Hooray!

I dress tzolia, dance zorba, yell oppa!
I eat souvlaki tarama, play bouzouki guitar
My religion is Greek Orthodox
But i feel like Pandora's Box

The Aegean twinkle shuffles my face
Thus swarming a placid pace full of
Grace, olive eyes, retsina rise
I can't disguise my Greek ties!

HARD BOILED SUSPENSE

Are you always dense or intense?
I may need to thoroughly cleanse
My slippery hard boiled suspense
I was a novice, in your province

I had enough of fake fudgy love
Fed up; with choosing n'loosing
It's akin to a lover's bruising
I'm tired of giving n'misgiving

Happiness is frothily calling
What else is steadily mauling
A new life is happily dawning
I'm not stalling just falling

are you fainting or wallpainting
Are you creating or anticipating
Remember to watch out for the bait
And pursue, a much healthier trait

I like to look at you everyday
And appreciate you in everyway
There's always a jolting descend
As you scuttlebutt to a closing end

HEARTACHING

Let me dry your tear
And bring you new cheer
I'll chill your every fear
Even when I'm not that near

You know i respect you
Like a brother and for
Me, there will be no other
I'll be an incredible lover

To steer you from any other
Every night: I'll make love
To you in my king sized bed
Comfortably, I'm cradle fed

Right under you're pose my
Body froze as my mind open
Closed, give me a break so i can
Indulge my fluffy chocolate cake

Why confuse the melody with the
Harmony? It's uncertain clarity
Let's go out on a date and mate
Don't risk defeat, just compete

You don't have to go through the
Agony; just to reach the ecstacy
I don't seek to be sadly mistaken
Or forsaken, I'm just heartaching

HELD YOU CLOSE

Held you close as i kissed you're cheek
In the pouring rain, it felt so good as
The sky wept away it's icy maze of hail
My blood was shivering chillingly frail

I never thought i would kiss you at all
I never thought i would hold you at all
I never thought i would feel you at all

But one day you know i did
That's when i grew from kid
Some say, i flipped my lid
But that's when i grew from kid

Those jealous eyes with their chunky lies
And hearts of woe tried to get between us
And our warming heavenly glow but we were
Strong and held on to what we always know

I **never** thought i would kiss you at all
I **never** thought i would hold you at all
I **never** thought i would feel you at all

But one day you know i did
That's when i grew from kid
Some **say,** i flipped my lid
But that's when i grew from kid

So many years have happily passed and there's
So much to show, with love in our hearts we've
Paved the way for eachother to grow, when you
Offer to help someone you're spirit shall flow

HONEYMOON

As i frolic in the midst of June
I smell your fresh sweet perfume
Just beneath the sparkling moon
All across the lake i bloom
I'm dancing like a racoon
And sing in n'out of tune

Beside the frog croaking lagoon
In between, the summery monsoon
    Underneath the honeymoon

How i like to see you soon
Under the crescent shining
Moon, with a tingle in my heart
I carefully aim at cupid's dart
As i dingle my precious worldly
Part mingling with dazzling art

Beside the frog croaking lagoon
In between, the summery monsoon
    Underneath the honeymoon

Think of all the nice things
We can probably see and do
When we happily hold eachother
And pleasantly say "I love you"
Imagine all the fun we could share
When we whisk ourselves without a care

HOWARD THE COWARD

I knew a police officer named Howard
My; he was a mighty big coward
He asked me for I.D.
So i produced bankcard and not a gun
That, he was happy to see

Walking down the dim city streets
Waving his club back and forth
He sensed violence out of the dark silence
A truck suddenly appeared
Seemingly out of nowhere

Without warning, it ran over Howard, our coward
That incident left a nasty stink in the air
In our municipality and elsewhere
"No great loss", shouted the barmaid
It's only Inspector Howard: the coward

The mother's club and Reverand O'Connor
Organized a church service in support
Of the town's number one coward
To some people's delight; the hospital caught fire
Alas! the fiery flames engulfed Chief Inspector Howard

All the town's people and
All the town's prayers
Couldn't put Howard back together again
I knew a police officer named Howard
My, he was a mighty big coward...

HOWEVER HUMBLE

I'm relieved to sigh
High up on the wings of
An albatross in the sky
I'll forever get on by

In cubicles of charm
I taste the bubbly wine
Feimented by expert vine
Maturing in rhapsody sine

Fraternally adopting from
Blossoming hive, orbiting
The cycle of inner mind's eye
Slowly ascending to ultimate i

Melancoly jolly regenerates as new
Cock's crow in dawn's dew, amongst
The winter's frost fading ice cube
However humble; life's like a tube

In a tide of vortex thought we're sought
Your love returns like a boomerang caught
Walking in footsteps of yesterday's dreams
What are today's ideals: tomorrow's schemes

HUMANITY IS POISONED BY LEGAL DRUGS

It's aching in head; so get ready for bed
It swallows so tight and it's ready to fight
Capsule for cold will dissolve, discomforts old
Measles and germs, you had your fill on my bill

You wined and dined on my anatomy
Now it's my turn to pine and sine
Purchasing everything will not do
For nothing stays forever true!

Everyone is possessed by these ills
Addictions that seek cheap thrills
Drugs are devil's thugs; for mugs
In your car, you fly off the tar

So in future buckle up extra safe and tight
Get a firm grip and pray you live the night
Don't become another statistic on the road
We all must carry a responsible heavy load

Alcohol makes you think you're bold, but
Once you're done you're left out in the cold
Death takes it's toll more than the dirty slugs
Humanity is poisoned by legal drugs!

HUMANITY'S RACES

I don't intend to lie behind a
False face, i seek to clear my
Name of all misery n'sad taste
And re-direct all of the waste

Time is ticking, life is flicking
We are the victims always licking
Wounds heal, hearts feel, bodies peel
What must we do? To feel lovingly new

Why try to wither my strong foundations
With your crumbling, vexing plantations
How can we resist? You're worldly class
It's upsetting like an earthquake blast

How can we fall flat on our faces
And end up, in exotic strange places
We must keep running with larger paces
And provide for all of humanity's races

HYPOTHETICAL PARADOX

Thank you very much, for you're magic touch
You look so delectable and super acceptable
You're beauty astounds n'profounds, many men
Will come from all races; and far off places

In childhood i was cradle fed, as i appeared
Almost half dead, i laid in bed n'often bled
The words of Shakespeare i quirkly read as i
Gently slept, but now I'm just weak and sore

My body bled as many tears i did shed
I couldn't even keep myself, well fed
It makes me spastic that your fantastic
I wish to jump on you're box and rewind

The clocks, love feels like a hypothetical paradox
Just stop the prognosis n'prescribe a prescription
To alleviate my addiction, like a cobra aiming not
To miss, the fruity lovely flavour is in your kiss

I CAN'T RECONSTRUCT THE PAST

I can't reconstruct the past
Even though it went forward fast
Xmas came late at my estate and i
Wish to thank you for a pleasant date

I feel so hearty that i want to party
So cut me loose from nasal slim noose
Shake off the mustard reclusive goose
It was a totally happy brilliant ball

With your latent love unwinding call
Put the seducing crystal ball in the
Royal Hall; as you foresee, whatever
Has to be, give me a glance or place

Me in a trance for sweet romance
Or a one-off manufactured stance
Like Fred Astaire I'll plurative dance
Fired up I'll enhance curative advance

My credo will absorb all the vile volition
In affirmative supposition it's abolition!
Our motto will be echoed in a new tomorrow
Decrepeting Down's syndrome disease sorrow

INCONSPICOUSLY CIRCUITOUS

As you scampered out of view
I flail away at you, peeling at
What we once knew, activating our
Splash down love whilst disengaging

The swarthy glissade piebald drum
Scaling the rungs of a yesteryear
Irascible flavours bring you near
Colonnading unfazed; without fear

Billowing the confidantes and smart
Tripthong minds as feinted adroitly
To the whirring of our hearts then
Indiscriminately bolstering my ego

Interpreting the pommel indecision
Ostensibly fathoming the applicable
Conglomerates, stringently corralled
Into inconspicuously circuitous passion

I HOPE I NEVER AWAKE

The closet door unwinds as
We silently slip thru time
Everything revolves n'evolves
Mellowing in the wisened soul

If you wish to leave me now
Then don't try to come back
You better keep walking on
The slippery railway track

Because you certainly don't belong
In my warm, rubbery, loving sack
Remember to jump off the highest
Bridge; you, two timing quack!

Was it love or tempting lust
That lay us both in the dust
There's not too many people
Whom you could really trust

If this is a dream?
Then i hope i never awake
I'll just smother myself
In you're fruity cake

ILLEGITIMATE GENIUS

If something is bothering you
Don't wear a heavy vest
Just get it off your chest
Then your heart can rest

At large, you camouflage
Your visage, then discharge
Illegitimate genius you are
No-one notices you from far

Ravish in glory, your a star
Einstein's catalyst on par
What can you create?
To sentence you HOORAH!!!

IMPASSE

Don't fandango with the sweet tooth mango
There's a suspicious multi faceless tango
Your vicious lithe is a unique technique
An impasse patented as a scoundrel's teeth

Audible, with a counterweight repository of
Contingent abject belief, the girl with the
High cheekbones and the gorgeous smile can
Surely lift up your will for a short while

The rawness of your quiver excites what i
Deliver; with churlish responsibilities i
Change my sweat stained shirt, sandles n'socks
Just because something has'nt been done before

It does'nt mean that it won't happen and more
Let's put the rubber to the road and unbirden
The heavy weighing load; if you have a coulisse
Copilot, you can take off and fly into the sky!

If you aim for the heliacal boom, your nerves will
Orbit the moon; A serrated mind cudgel's the fumes
Friar's spatter blessings with finger ring dressings
I pallid write my vivid inconsolable hostage memoirs

That sit on the bloody barbed wire lacerating fence
In all the heedy commotion i lose all natural sense
It's a vertigo of emotion dense; ripping my carotid
Vein and repeating giddy concocting feverpitch pain

INSCRUTABLY INSIPID

Don't beat around the bush, just push
I'm very curious so don't make me furious
You seem superbly luxurious with you're fancy
Orangy pastel nail polish n'silvery dark eyeliner

You look much finer than any other fashion designer
The sweet pouty lips n'pleasant tasting pseudo kiss
All wrapped up in natural bliss; so how can you miss
Do you prefer the cardiograph, or the perspectograph

The discerning narrowing pathway is inscrutably insipid
It's so defeasibly ineffable and chillingly inseperable
You're fundamentals are highlighting like neon rentals
Tippling then contravening, unorthodox bare essentials

If you surgically remove you're womb then you cannot
Reproduce; you might as well lock yourself in a tomb
Can you remind yourself of any disorders of the mind
Because your so introverted n'find it hard to unwind

INSTINCT IS EMOTION

I want you forever
And not only a day
I'll cherish you better
If your with me to stay

Instinct is emotion
As loyal as devotion
Linger sibling scent
Which is heaven sent

You once roamed the streets
With cold feet, little to eat
You've advanced spectator's seat
From last to first eccentric feat

Empatically yell to show your swell
Illuminate fable, on high wire cable
Evasive pirates plunged into deep sea
Passion plea still free for all to see

Dynamic duality is your flexible key
In emergency you purport bronze knee
Rambling on it's a bit of fluff song
Fugacious sequacious mystique is non

INTOLERABLE ALIBI'S

I was stock taking, thru the yearly emblements
And placed them in a pile of sostenuto sorosis
I was pleasantly impressed and highly immersed
I felt sandblasted and extremely flabbergasted

My heart always had a soft spot for sweet cute lovable
Innocently attractive you, you're liposuctioned thighs
Airbrush lies and intolerable alibi's, were no surprise
Such a puritanical style and slightly incredulous smile

You left you're softly indecorous mark, closely after dark
As i blindly tripped into the duck filled pond in the park
I felt like i was semantically launched in Noah's Ark, but
I was knocked out by love's arrow like a senseless sparrow

IRRESISTABLE PEEK

Even when i appear as a dove
Your still afraid to truly love
You must have been hurt bad before
Hurriedly you close compartment door

I know you can blow me away
With your rauncy vibrant ray
How tender n'amorous must i stay
To be seduced by your buttock way?

A broken heart can be mended
And timid fiery passion blended
Your so sleek as i watch you sleep
I just have to have irresistable peek

IS THAT A RAINBOW

Is that a rainbow shining true
Is that a rainbow coming thru
All those beautiful colours
They remind me of lovable you
Is that a rainbow coming thru

I have struggled so hard most of my life
Much turmoil and suffering, were my wife
Felt hardships and pain, it wasn't right
Nothing justified my existence in strife
I had to hold on till things got alright

Is that a rainbow shining true
Is that a rainbow coming thru
All those beautiful colours
They remind me of lovable you
Is that a rainbow coming thru

Let's talk about heaven while we listen
To the cries of all the starving little
Children dying before our helpless eyes
We need to take charge with firm action
To steer away from any delayed reaction

Is that a rainbow shining true
Is that a rainbow coming thru
All those beautiful colours
They remind me of lovable you
Is that a rainbow coming thru

JINGLE JANGLE

I wink with my eye
You sink with your sigh
My mind is far too wide
Your love clings like tide

Darling, why can't you make me
Jingle jangle: twingle twangle?
The way you do when you bang my
Gland with extra tang, sweet fang

It's not often i get this vibration
So let's not avoid Miss sensation
It's a very sexy warm manifestation
And a rare blend of love fixation

Why don't you give me vitamin lotion or
Bodybuilding potion so i can carve out
My nerve n'fibre motion: thus flex our
New found muscle notion; what commotion

Please don't tease me anymore
Please, please me more n'more
Darling, why can't you make me
Jingle jangle: twingle twangle?

JUST FOR YOU

I remember when we first locked eyes, it
Desirably bedazzled, my heart's surprise
Strolling through the rose perfumed garden
Amidst the dim twilight, bubbling fountain

You cannot even begin to sense
How terribly fond, i was of you
You blessed my soul as i happily
Never ever knew; i looked up with

The utmost respect for you, i would have
Easily attempted everything and anything
Just for you, i truly wanted to live n'die
For you, but the same was just never true!

JUST GIVE ME ANOTHER TRY

Now I'm learning awful fast that love
Doesn't always last or come back vast
I don't want to super rush it in case
I besom crush it or suicidal slush it

Everyone is individually new, leaving
Jarring glue not always remaining true
We all aren't the same and aim to hunt
Different game maybe not quite so tame

Why do you play the jew's harp
And slice me nice but so sharp
Do i harken to the angel's harp
To ascend from purgatory's raft

From Kilimanjaro to Fuji I'll yell
And beg to be lifted up from Hell
With a purifying isapostolic smell
I can hear the free resonant bell

You can't forgive with critical eye
Or distinguish truth from lie
You only cause yourself to cry
When you won't listen to my why

Don't wonder why just give me another try!

KASTORIA

Kastoria is a town unlike any other town
It is surrounded by a lake all around:
I Won't go into detail about this illustrious
Town, or i shall have to fill novels abound

The wind passes it's buildings yet sounds
Different notes, like a tune in the woods
Crackling in verse, Kastoria appears sunburst
It's relics n'arts are it's crafts of the past

Gold may be found just lurking around
Some dig deep' without a lucky strike
Others search in day and others at night
It's active volcano lies dormant inside!

Like the inhabitants furnace pride
Seesawing as a happy carousel ride
A vernacular chemistry of Byzantine side
Captured by the Romans in two hundred B.C.

It fell to the Normans in ten-eighty-three
Betrayed to the Serbs in thirteen-thirty-one
Half a century later the Turks invaded sum
In nineteen-thirteen the Greeks finally won!

Fisheries float upon the mega lake while
Limestone mountains and chestnut orchids
Appease the lake, foxes n'bears roam till
Late, tourists adore this enhancing state

The mayor now wants to set up a fund, so they
Can dredge out the seven metres of muck n'mud
The environment must be overhauled, reshaped and
Redone, the nuissance of pollution must be none!

Churches align practically every street corner
They're highly decorated with frescoes inside;
When Hitler's army marched through neighbouring
Towns, footpaths cracked, while buildings bowed

When they got to Kastoria the frozen lake opened
And in they bowed. 8oy, what a sight! They froze
More than fright, collating a miserable plight
We still don't commiserate their fearful fight

These days it's involved in more constructive
Things, such as exporting furs and skins
What the future lies i do not know
Nostradamus did not tell me so

KNIGHTS OF THE ROUND TABLE

In King Arthur's land lived more than a man
Who preached his thoughts with courage bland
Chivalry and Pendragon rage from sea to sand
All the knights wore gold in heart and hand

Stories of them have been told of
When they were virtous young n'bold
Thru legend centuries myths are old
What really was their mystical role?

Was it dignified to see culprit dole?
In search for the elusive Holy Grail
Their effort grew fierce weary frail
Scrounging for clues they had blues!

How could they forsake wise views?
Even at feasts they acted as beasts
Wearing gowns covered by nice frowns
Guinevere swiftly treads new grounds

When she jest's, it's best to not rest
Don't be dazzled by her sensual breast
Lady of the Lake and Morgan Le Fay why
Not caress and bless my seasoned guest

Wave your censer to exorcise the pest
Arthur has to rule bipartisan realm
Nimiane weaves wicked cursing spell
Mandrake Merlin knows it all too well

Dragonlord brandishes Excalibur bell and
The Virgin Mary on his shield does tell
That christianity has pierced pagan shell
Free Britain from the barbaric Saxon cell

Merlin, what destiny can you forsee?
Extrapolating from the future's tree
Can England reign for generations free?
Or struggle in agony; above n'beyond me

Lancelot you've deceived your church plot
So you now must be banished from our lot;
Fair maidens toy to quench your surmounting
Layback drench, what a filthy odour stench!

Overlooked by a cosmic gable presided by
The meek n'soul righteous christian able
Knights of the round table swore allegiance
To Camelot safe stable seeking many a fable

Whilst uniting England with electric cable
A damsel in distress was prized like sable
When jousting and toasting at honour table
Were they rough n'ready willing or disabled?

LAY OFF THE TART

Your as skinny as a rake shiver
N'quake like an excessive flake
I thought we nearly had it made
But you hit with excoriate spade

Thus splitting my acolyte ego aid
Our situation blocked; conclusive
Hastly i defaulted achene elusive
As our love was divided diffusive

With the slip of the Freudian tongue
And juxtaposition of the Jungian arm
Libido is an increase state of ego aid
Coming from instincts that are man made

I deposited firm my jelly safe sperm
But you insisted it lay full of germ
Please decongest your part in clean art
Let's start apart and lay off the tart!

LEND ME YOUR HAND

I knew a man who lived by the sea
He worshipped it till eternity
I visited him very regularly
As he preached his philosophy

"Lend me your hand"
And I'll be your guiding hand
Together we'll do whatever
We can!

LIBIDO CHANT

Problems are facing us in every age
Decorating themselves as cloudy days
Behind each mask lies a face
That eagerly yearns to escape

From life's unexpectancies; hooded capes
In future we'll use fluent tapes
Learning values, learning games
Living with situations offered by chance

Growing intelligently whilst in a trance
Discovering fate beyond glance
And purpose that will enhance
Aiming for aims without any circumstance

Fathoming the sanctum of the libido chant
Prophets are restricted by the shunt in time
Being indispensable in teaching rhyme, rolling
With life's slippery wheel don't forget to alter

Destiny at will!••• Masterpieces of our heritage
Will never decay; they won't consume a reason to
Wither away, thus revealing wisdom to me now and
Only now, challenging trails bewail, ego's frail

LISA VISA

On the tower of Pisa
Lisa looked at her visa
Remembering hotel rooms she
Glanced back at potential grooms

And recalled how her mama
Chased them with wet broom
It made her go boom! when the
Sleazy lads messed up her room

After that blue she was knocked
In-two n'in bed with the flu!
Her mum asked; How do you do?
Lisa still sits on tower Pisa

Gauging her eccentric seizure
Eclipsing all logical fissure
Supplying nutrients tease her
Virtue and honour please her!

Eating pizza, laughing n'snorting
Rotating notions of love courting
Forever sorting, cupid supporting
Cavorting to stranger's soughting

On the tower of Pisa
Sits lovely Lisa, waiting
For the right geezer to
Extend her loving visa!

LITTLE LOST COLOURED BALL

My little lost coloured ball
Where did you bounce and
Where did you crawl
Did someone break you're fall

Did you show your sorry face
At the amusement hall?
Did anyone offer to wash the dirt
N'smut, when you fell in the hole

My little lost coloured ball
Were you tossed out in the gutter
And sadly left weeping alone
Freaking out and far from home

Did anyone hear you despairingly moan
Were you trampled over mud n'bone
Did you manage to find a new home
Did you roll away with the stones

My little lost coloured ball
Where did you bounce and
Where did you crawl
Did you end up at the royal ball

LOOK FORWARD

How are you sleeping my pretty darling
Have you amassed much fortune and fame
Are you still writing you're life long
Diary, or are you pursuing another aim

With tit for tat we will simply bat
We'll replace monoxide with dioxide
And bring back some flora and fauna
Lopping around the very next corner

What do i have to say to excite you
Why do i have to play to ignite you
Is there something i can do to delight you
You're ballooning belly; is just above you

My mind is like a sharp razor blade
Marvelling at the way the siren's sway
Look forward and see the world around you
It's many wonders will literally astound you

LOSE GRIP

Gibbons swing blackbirds sing
I love you, and you love me
That's the way it has to be
I'm so serene, happy n'keen

As i crashed on your slate
I was put in a sick state
I observed the way you
Prior pushed me around

You laughed at my acrobatic gown
You made me foolish; utter clown
Renouncing our bittersweet pound
I thought you were God come down

I'm trapped in your poison prison
Where the ceiling filters treason
Later or sooner, you'll lose grip
Then you'll trip, slip, drip drip

LOST FOR WORDS

What can i say to take you away on this
Awkward day? I'm lost for words so I'll
Have to pray: Never in my life have i
Felt this way! In a minute there will

Dawn a brand new day so look upon me gay
Forget the worries that beseech your pay
I'll look after you like gold so stay by
Me till old! I know you've probably heard

That line before and the stock is depleting
From my store but I'm really Lost for Words

So i can't say anymore!

LOVE TUNNEL

I try to run back to you
Just want to know why we're thru
How can you be so dismal dense
When I'm on fire, intense

How can you look so pathetic?
When all i want is to be alive, energetic
Why should you try to run n'hide?
When all you own is attention, pride

Which you can no longer ride
Whatever you do, whatever you say
You can't obliterate the truth
Because it's there to stay

Your eyes try hard to hook
With a perplexing puzzled look
Your harder to read than a book
Are you really serious or plain delirious?

I don't have a long enough funnel
So don't bait me in your love tunnel
Shall we kiss and start again?
Or slap cheeks, break heart, end!

MAGIC SPELL

Your spirit is full of neglected zeal
So utterly abhorrent you must feel
Of the barging modicum living seal
Outrageous, contagious is your appeal

Witches cast their magic spell
Wizards conjure powers from Hell
Eyes of toads and lizards too
Legs of frogs in purple blue

Go hand in hand to make
The witches brew; undeterred is
The wizard's flu: this generation
Lacks the diplomatic view!

In the cauldron bubbles bake
The potion fizzles like a flake
The tiu'ot reads it's no mistake
Black cat pur's the crystal fate

The serpent sings with gorgon rings!
The full moon spins it's amulet pins
The voodoo doll is not a hallow role
This possessive spell i cannot extol

MAKE MODEL YEAR
LIQUID ENGINEER

I work behind a busy counter in an
Automative store; the hour glass i
Can't ignore, everything is wanted
Even next door right away and more

The parts and junk that surround me
I cannot deplore: What a lax chore?
While servicing my customers i offer
Whatever knowledge like hot porridge

My advice is usually heeded in advance
And welcomed in perplexing circumstance
I don't claim to be a graduate mechanic
Or a whizz-kid industrious spanner manic

So when the motor cars get awful sick
I can wind them up; to clockwork tick
My shifty hands propose to do the trick
Watch out in case you get a nasty prick

I'm supposed to know all the numbers of
Moving nuts, bolts, and gears for every
Vehicle that has been made from all over
The world in more than fofty past years!

I'm not a marvellous liquid engineer
Just a soft spoken meticulous peer
That tries to stay away from the beer
And serve his customers with a cheer!

I'm often hailed as the lubricating clone
Of the danger zone; luckily i don't drone
With the pence, instead I'm flattered by
Humility n'sense, i do bounce back tense

My life would be a scout like pleasure
An I'd harmonically sing from ear to ear
If the customer would remember to tell me
The correct make, model, and the year!

MAKE UP YOU'RE MIND

we had a very interesting conversation
Which lasted between station to station
It's probably hard for you to understand
That i respected you more than anyother man

Nevertheless I'll just lay in my satin bed
And rest my waterlogged nerve racking head
You know you're ex-boyfriend, is a baboon
So why do you still feed his silver spoon

He's on the brink, properly he cannot think
Don't make me acromanic by submissive panic
Listen *i* won't go after you all of the time
So please, hurry up and make up you're mind

MAKE YOU MINE

Baby when i saw you i realised that
What i had to do was make you mine
Purr as you talk like pussy's walk
Even though your sly you tell no lie

Your my Stabat Mater on a silver platter
When you bend like a fig to idle chatter
My mind bombards like cuccumber splatter
As you fall so free like an apple from a

Tree, it's Newton's Law to me, momentously
In a sharp decision spurned with precision
You perceived division from crystal vision
Churning blackened steel crumbles away our

Zeal, your cleansing sense trickles down
Like rain from cloud a very robust sound
Making me imagine profound in a rotating
Mound, applying a strategy of a newfound

I can't go on to describe my fleeting mind
Or express my adoring love for you thru time
I'll drink your wine I'll suck you just fine
I know all I'v got to do, is make you mine

MEANINGFULLY MERGE

Mentally i reject torpid young
Sentimentally you bite my worn
Out tongue pumping grotty grime
Dispensing amazing jitter rhyme

Upon question time just mime
Don't thumble, stolid chime
Shattered blow; stunted flow
Disinfected room to afterglow

The magic of love we shared
Didn't remain intact paired
What parenthetic paragon
Do you want me to portray?

I need a parasol to shaden the ray
An amiable life to blot out the grey
Is there an explanation palpitation
Or another reason to seek citation?

Meandering through mediocre junk pile
Your trophy smile excited for a while
Now i must carefully contribute much
Greater tribute to your rare attribute

Resilient be my affliction and diligent
Our work load addiction; alter friction
With soft diction we should meaningfully
Merge to onward surge, in love submerge!

MELTING IN THE SUN

You can't give up, just
Because of wrong choice
I fell asleep with your
Bubbly soft sweet voice

And when the morning sun
Awakens my dribling face
I'll meet my future darling
Wallowing in heavenly grace

Our shadows keep connecting
In scented, burning candles
Paning our minds far out
Into intergalactic space

Your body resembles ice cream
Enjoyably, melting in the sun
As you eagerly lick your love
Pleasantly having so much fun

MERE MORTAL MAN

I'm just a mere mortal man
I can't summon spirit hand
How can i fight off land? In
Non ecclesiastical quicksand

Is father Zeus a retired recluse?
Can he intercede cackling goose
And cheat the hangman's noose?
What pentameter is of use?

With a sirocco spray
Can i be whisked away
To a renaissance day where
Botticelli and Michelangelo play?

Beyond the realms of reasoning
Lie many different seasoning
A man must do what he can before
He's denied everything; And?....

MIRROR MIRROR

Mirror mirror on the wall
Whose the fairest of them all
I seek a man so strong n'tall
Will i loose my slipper at the ball

Mirror mirror on the wall
Do i hear prince charming's call
Will i fall in love at all?
Am i up for hhe royal call

Mirror mirror on the wall
Am i short or just too tall
Can you catch me when i fall
Will a vampire suck my blood at all

Mirror mirror on the wall
I'm sick of drinking bonnyclabber
How i wish to drown in bubbly lather
Go and fetch me the golden dagger

Mirror mirror on the wall
Whose the fairest of them all
Is it me or some other girl you love
Does she fit like a glove?

MISSING YOU'RE PASSIONATE KISS

I can't go on, like this
Missing you're passionate kiss
My heart less often bangs
Without you're satisfying tang

Like a lofty sombrero i do hang
As the prison bell manacle rang
Can you spare me this dimple rash
My one and only, comfy pretty Ash

It don't matter what you say
Or do' Love was made for two
We must gain a full frontal view
Without an eruptive exigent clue

How many hang up's are bothering you
You're like a rotting corpse sipping
Irish stew; to be sincerely true we
Must see it thru: So how do you do?

Tantamount n'paramount, is my love
For you, it's always been you, you
And only you, no one else will ever do
No one can ever take the place of you!

I miss kissing, those luscious lips, caviar
Dips, champagne sips, late night flips, ego
Trips; I can't go on like this
Missing you're passionate kiss

MOTIVE I

It's magic when your eyes meet mine
We feel love so sweet and fry
Unlike uncouth words of envy dry

I'm like an escapologist that's just
Wiggled his way out of a straitjacket
Only to serve from a broken tennis racket

The Eiffel Tower renounces your previous
Reign of despicable unpleasant clad cower
Everything became muddled-up fumigating sour

Einstein illuminated the relative power
Valentino heralded the sexy flower
Sartre retained the existentialist hour

My appointment with you is like
Having a blood transfusion as the
Laboratory is besieged with confusion

That's why now I'll chew the betel nut
And figure out a way out of this rut
Hold on I'm heading for the right stuff

I hear thunderclap from the starlit sky
Copyright forbids plagarism by acapella i
It's not at all a measely drawn out story

So we cannot rob you of prestigious glory
Our drawcard is the motive i
A culprit of you and eye

MOURN PARADOXES

Don't delve on the past
As if it were the present
Foolish be you no more;
We must accept the facts

No matter how elusive or conclusive
Pretentious the score, indecisions
Are many in this world of mounting
Confusion, illusion and hate. How can

People complain when they're the bait
The bait? What a corruptable fate!
Idols of chance, aren't emulating
True values to our society's bread

It's all turned degenerate, stale, dead
Our body's born for barter, pawn n'bled
Social evils sacrifice exorbitantly high
As the flaring glaring midday desert sky

Torchbearing mornings fade to hotter noon
We mourn paradoxes all too soon; so bloom
Finally, i gazed at my self created maze
I sure felt dazed and spoon fed rnalaised

MURDERED BY TALK

It's ten to two and you've nothing to do?
They start from one and advance to none!
As long as they're there, that's all i care
Talk about money if your bare, some don't dare

Murdered by talk, where do you walk?
Smart in your language, dumb in mine
Man, i don't really mind; bethought of a
Job so kind, good friends match your test

Like buzzards in a nest, sweet and blessed
What miracle has made you ultimately best?
Gyres of air tilter through my chair
Fondling pigeons play upon your hair

Why dilly dally with a snazzy snare?
It's a turning point flashpoint dare
Raving on, all is non; when you lose
The score, don't grin at me for more

MUSHY ALIBI'S

I never ever thought I'd find a girl like you
I felt so inconspicuous as though my life was
Through, but now i have plenty to say then do
Aesthetically you renounced, your weathercock

Lies and evenly handed slushy, mushy alibi's
I grin to the teeth, with your relative ties
Is there a trick to your treat? amazing feat
Or a sought out companion, so funny and neat

Nostalgically i remained sore, inhibiting my
Teeny weeny blistering paw and for what more
I felt so solemnly divine even though i bled
And suffered unkind; meandering with my time

MY BURNING YEARN

The dark and eerie sound of night, held
A deep unearthly silence, in the strange
Heat of it, "sensing a show-down", i then
Mudwrestled myself whilst listening to the

Looney tunes of fallen crickets and fresh
Water frogs; after running out of the hut
And diving into murky waters of the filthy
Polluted lake just to escape the inner bite

Of my burning yearn, i gaped at the vast black
Celestial Andromeda sky where flickering stars
Appeared as key holes of a strange but universal
Sanctum, trying to distil into omniscient fusion

While uncluttering the blistering confusion, an old
Epitaph thrives on illusion; such awesome diffusion
Allocating my conscious mind and puzzling everything
Which was previously explainable to everyday mankind

MY FANTASIES HAVE ALL DECAYED

You laugh at me and also cry and lie
You tease then please all night long
I sit and stare then look at all the
Fussy people rushing down the street

They're far too busy, looking up
So they miss out on the trophy cup
A thought echoes in my meek mind
Which person combines true reality

My fantasies have all decayed
Like expectations that haven't stayed
And if you should not like my style then
Don't mind this one, who speaks out loud

You notice a handsome stranger sitting there
Tickling his shoulder length wavy brown hair
He stops to see your freshly painted face n'hair
He captures a fragile glimpse, of affection rare

He appeals to your semi tinted, sunscreen eyes
Reminiscing at the backlog of bittersweet lies
Whisking through merits of his highlight life
Snivelling at the bounty of mediocrity strike

He fills you with drinks and antics deploring
Scenario semantics, you grin n'wonder if it's
Right? For lonely broken hearts to feel shame
Reflecting back now we know this awesome game

MY LADY

I wish to glance at your frown
I just want to wear your gown
May i please put on my crown
Do i sense you now going down

My lady weeps away in the night
And dreams of a love that's right
If i start my fast flight
Will it comfort her last plight?

Do i remain a mystery
Or a bird flying free
How shall i try to rub
Sad disgrace from my tub

I power sail to unruffled sea
To escape this love tormenting me
In a foreign land and time, maybe
I can surface from this crime?

My lady sleeps alone in the night
There's no one there to hold her tight
I'm so far away i can't even write
It's such a pity it don't seem right

MYSTICAL AND MAGICAL

Mystical and magical you befell on me
And swept my face with a fresh breeze
Clouding my eyes in your naked stream
Appearing so bright by being so green

Mystical and magical you gazed upon me
Cleansing my soul with sensous whiffle
Rejoicing my mind so swiftly and right
Causing me to faint, for a short while

When renewing my auspicious style
Preening, amiable then worthwhile
In a web of anger you ended it all
The beginning of; our eternal ball

NEVER MIND MY BLEEDING MIND

In another time and place i felt
The memory which i trace no more
A stone broke, the •urface of the pond
It brought ripples of tears to my lame
Lonely hurting heart one more sad time

Never mind my bleeding mind
For i learnt from your disguise
In a fantasy world; that rhymes
Were we not meant for eachother?
At least for a dimension in time

ONE AND ONLY WAY

You'll be my night
You'll be my day
You'll be my one
And only way

I'll love you once
I'll love you twice
I'll love you till
I'm dead with lice

You'll be my pride
You'll be my joy
You'll be my one
Spectacular toy

I'll love you first
I'll love you last
I'll love you till
I'm under glass

You'll be my night
You'll be my day
You'll be my one
And only way!

ONSLAUGHT

On the way to the cemetery where i do
Give my respect to valiant dead lives
I recall perilous wasteful apocalyptic war
General's collars appeared virginal bright

As war ravaged they reflected brittle light
The gloss shrivelled n'cost with lives lost
White man did not honour the great spirit
Homage was not given to it on sacred days

Taunted in love with greed there was no need
Zenith zest was man's fervid urge; with extreme
Arsenal he surged, fractured skulls bones n'jaws
Lay all along the outdoor: today's birds of prey

The mighty eagle, vulture, hawk, tend to toll the
Extinct roll, thus licking ageing bone, on open
Plains bison once roamed furiously free but now
They bear no offspring to passionately stand free

Pleasant: it's not for the naive eye naked to see
The onslaught was catastrophic n'ploughed on thee
A calamity equalling biblical proportions in knee
Deep blood n'sweaty eyes, cannot still camouflage

The compounding lust and counterfeit trust reduced
The bison to rodent disgust! The buffalo were shot
Down for their meat n'hides; boasting white settlers
Sport n'prize and Indian chiefs stature size, before

Medicine man's ceremonial vies, which ancient magic
Now defies, to decimate an animal weighing a ton
Just for fun, was the cowboy's rattle and hum
It wasn't a fair game just deliberate dumb

The largest population of massive brute
On earth, simply was denied it's worth
Sixty million innocent, sentenced dead
Without any criminal crime

Without a justifiable jury
Without a pleading plea
No one there to help, not even me!
How many other species will there be left to be?

PEACE ERUPTING SWING

I squeeze you very densely because
I admire you, so utterly immensely
I cherish you more, than any other
Living thing and sumptuously drink

Fresh water from your clear spring
To exhibit such a perfecting sting
Flowing in an outward, backward sling
What a marvellous sugary exotic fling

The freshness of nature's purity grin
Humans, animals, insects n'marsupials
Unite to sing: in a jubilant voice of
Spring, wow what peace erupting swing

PEACE ON EARTH

How many lives, have been lost?
Don't you think it's a sad cost
To live with war and decay
And blow our planet away

Son, you've grown up big n'strong
Don't you think it's rather wrong
To be shipped away, for so long
And miss out on love forever on

All i wish, All i say
Is for peace on earth to come today
All i want, All i pray
Is for peace on earth to reign n'stay

I see beggars crying in the streets
Praying for happier days to be beat
Take the smoulder from they're eyes
Enlighten their souls, to the skies

Like bitten lips, whirling from the
Pain, the search for love lies in vain
Dazzling with ease, you're trying to please
Life can be a tease, swept away by the breeze

All i wish, All i say
Is for peace on earth to come today
All i want, All i pray
Is for peace on earth to reign n'stay

PENANCE

Skyscrapers restrict sunlight reducing
Warmth, can you stand when it's so
Easy to fall from the laxing call?
Why be a fuss-pot at the senior's ball

In future's time, foreign action will
Mend your grind; they'll be a contract
For you to sign, in blood and red wine
It'll be a healthy treaty for my mind

Jack of all trades and master of some
I am as the tide of the oceanic crest
Scouring the earth for a love that's best
Seeking restlessly, for my undying quest!

I hover for a kingdom to be a welcomed guest
Needless to say it's an ecclesiastical test
Touching your penance nest, i unduly rest
My life is a soap-opera treasure chest!

PERFECT STATE

You can have the irradianting upperhand
As long as i can play in your safe land
I'll try to be loyal just like you want
Cause you're my royal, just like i long

I like you and you like me
That's the way it's supposed to be
Our love stems like the oak tree
Growing big n'strong for all to see

We don't need to pretend anymore
And use lies for bait; we have no
Time for dead deeds and past mistakes
Just bring forward a clear perfect state

PERPETUAL SCHEME

The seductive lady in my dream
Had a totally perpetual scheme
To overthrow our love so clean
Quickly n'serene, mock obscene

I know the strange way you must feel
That's why i unjustly, wish to steal
Congragulations and sweet exhiltations
You deceive very badly yet i crave for

You madly, I'm very jealous of him
And i want to throw him in the bin
Our love has headed way off course
Landing in a pudency, of discourse

The flutter n'the putter has gladly
Dissolved, shall i fetch the bex or
Would you prefer sex? I know you're very
Choosy but I'm not a cheap little floosy

PERPLEXING ILLUSION

As i ran after some summer fun
I thought I'd fire up like a gun
And bounce off the flaming sun
I'd rather get washed up; in the

Flood then drizzily drown, in mediocre mud
You're aching to disconnect from past sorrow
And happily looking for a brighter tomorrow
There must be a simple solution for you're

Venomous confusion so just ayoid the perplexing
Illusion, which sparks the contaminating fusion
Would you rather have a lot of a little, or a
Little of a lot? What riddles have you forgot

PERSIST IN CIST

Are you going to make me
Fall in love with you?
Refute everything old for new
Forsake anything else but you

If that's the case, I'll put you
In your place and plant firm base
Mysterious loom composes flat tune
Culture shock doesn't knock it just

Flocks; bluntly it will wallop
Your trollop indescribable dollop
Obtrusively read on Zosimus art page
Dominion cult age refuge inundated cage

Zucchetto was branded divinely of grace
It's chapel warm and tender with embrace
Simon Magus rest your face; magic exit is
The divine list quoted to persist in cist

PERTAIN TO ENTERTAIN

I want to go home to bed all alone
Not listen to phone or needles sown
Look, i just wanted us to be friends
And not have any measureable pretends

I'd cling to you if you'd fling to me
I'd squash every ounce of angry pain
Dry you clean from the marauding rain
Under mansard-roof we'll ease the fain

Then I'll mediate the mud and grease
From your fast moving bullet strain
Catapulting it on board express train
Evicting the hurt and nauseating stain

I'd pertain to entertain your every vein
By amusing it with responsible circulatory
Pre-select rotating oblate portable state
Proliferating wealth fete at abundant rate

We'll order caviar and dine like a star
We'll drink champagne n'forget the rain
In Spain, I'll serve you pheasant under
Glass and denounce the bourgeois class!

PETALS GREEN

I was floating high on a white rubicon of hot love
My wings of shiny crystal, innocently had surfaced
All of the chummy fun, you niggle with small ronage
Are you expecting to pocket, a much larger coinage?

In a shrewd sharp instance, i thought i would feel
You suddenly rise up happily from the petals green
You're hungry zephyr eyes do solemnly glean, holding
You up in total esteem! So how do you let off steam?

PINK MINK

Your foxy stare filters with glare
Your rosy cheeks peak pubic hair
Rising shadows laser beams naked
Cringing cumbersome, subtle serene

My mind has to part it's oasis art
Pink mink is what you upfront wear
When you want me to beckon beware
Forget the mundane artificial lair

Explicably dazzle luscious flair
Of fickle tinsel, granite bare
How I'd love to wrap n'tap your
Inner psyche to a mammoth fluffy

Hype, thus spook your inner sight
In humble delight, flutter blunt
To exorbitant punt: grunt; pink mink
Doesn't stink it just makes me think blink!

POINT OF PAIN

Why don't i feel the way
I used to pleasantly feel?
Can you revive me with your
Steamy love, aphrodisic pill?

You really ought to examine my
Loving feelings for you, but
Emotionally you're just too weak
That's why you can't reach the peak

If your love for me were a desert
Then you would see· only the sand
If my love for you were an ocean
They're would be nowhere to land

Like a jobber selling in vain
We must pass the point of pain
In order to acquire true gain
Some people are scared of fame

Winners aren't afraid to lose
Even though they don't always
Have righteous, clear cut views
So what's the latest urban news?

POSITIVE STATE BRIGHTER FATE

We must orate a positive state
To secure a much brighter fate
Then scrub out all the nasty hate
Not feed spastic from plastic plate

We will remedy all disease oblate
With a germ free cleaning out rate
A show of surgical hygiene not late
To minimize the genetic science bait

We cannot frustrate the timely date
When we orchestrate a healthier mate
We can create a duplex perching state
And universally secure a brighter fate

PRE-POSTHUMOUS BELL

I know that you need a friend
Someone that you can depend on
When life bends lonely and sad
Everyone hides something away

And does'nt wish to recall it
Even till their last dying day
Ashamedly they just steer astray
From life's hurt n'prejudice way

Are you still restricted by the bind in
Ego's shell? Break free, from it's spell
I'm sure they'll be much to tell; revel!
What if we ring the pre-posthumous bell?

PREVAIL THRU THE HAIL

I hear you weeping sadly far from home
I see you trembling madly upon soft foam
Will you call me from your new mobile phone
Why spend another night in the bumbledom zone

You're eyes cook so cold when you forfeit all
The gold! What epitaph shall nervously unfold
We don't have to wait, to clutch at life till
We're old, you're bohemian lifestyle explores

The array of dualism, cubism, n'the various entities
Of existentialism; you're attolent mindset is sealed
In bolection, as your fingers waltz frantically over
The piano keys, but your compositions fail to please

So how do you appease? Can you play something melodious for me?
You look so utterly pale, so let's alleviate your incurable ail
You're logic needs conviction, as your life is free of restriction
Let's set forth upon a new exciting sail, to prevail thru the hail

PRIMA DONNA BEAMS

I need all the love, i can get
For without it I'm flirting on a
Highwire net, i don't wish to be a
Casualty on a hunter's lame duck bet

You're my cute mini protective pet
Shunning publicity by charming the
Paparazzi set; i quickly sheltered
Something inside that i had to hide

You instilled love so warm and tried
Like soothing waters in a lagoon tide
You answered all of my silly little dreams
Anticipating healing with prima donna beams

PROCEED AND EXCEED

I was so scared, to have a relationship with you
Because i knew i couldn't steer the sinking ship
I was no captain hero, flying up from ground zero
We progressed to a higher arch without any starch

How grateful was i when you drove out the filth
That spilled in my soul, n'drilled into my hole
The vermin shot me cold then it crippled me bold
I squealed like a cat, i am truly sorry for that

I couldn't even give you a lousy, little drip drop
From my overfilled street corner delicatessen shop
If we can only take heed we can proceed and exceed
In front of mankind we can leave the rocket behind

PROUD ESTEEM

I watched you dance and was in a trance
The things you do, manifest as true
Can i be sure, what I'm living for?
So sweet the girl i never knew

Could change my ardent view
Like prophets few, stubborn too
I crackled glimp, flicked a freckle
Then she turned into Mrs. Jeckle

You are a child of the night
Creep n'hiss amongst disco lights
What pagan features loll within?
Don't take my soul and win!

They told me that spirits were
Afraid of the cross, but when i
Crossed your path you were the boss
Such a feeling i never felt before:

I'm weak and helpless; i crave no more
Stop all the gore, please don't lift
My brain far out inter-galactic space
I'm only a specimen of the human race

I'll be your servant so grateful to please
Put bubbles in your bath, cajole with ease
Scrub you soft, clean with silky steam
That will be my enviable, proud esteem

PURITY LAUNCH

My stirring emotion performs many wonders
As your gentle touch, stealthily plunders
My heartbeat rampantly sizzles and fries
When I'm near you my dear all my worries

Silently disappear, i let off a happy
Immortal cheer, I'll be your fury pet
So don't you fret just place your bet
I'll jostle you; on the prodigy porch

Then electrify your contentious torch
You're zestfulness is eager n'staunch
Like a hurricane you viciously raunch
Mortifying the pristine purity launch

QUIDDLE FATIGUE

If your a jigsaw puzzle
I'm a dog without a muzzle
Don't be a backstabbing bitch
With a nervous twitch; snitch

You may feel like a doormat
Yet I'm a belated disseize brat
If we adopt the prudent delphi technique
We'll eliminate the subculture quiddle fatigue

Things don't always go according to plan
That's why we should stratify our clan
We must be able to interpret something
Before we can fully understand it!

When we launch our tour de force
We'll rumble like the myths of Norse
I'm not a malicious intruder; but a
Verbal commuter, in status quo Bermuda

Anyone can juggle a few balls in the air
But the magic trick is to keep them there
I must protest and detest at this trip tray
Defacto glare; coupled with a monotonous stare

RAPIDLY CHANGING

I don't confess to know everything, so i cannot
Declare to pack a sting on an unflappable fling
You won't try to build a rainbow bridge to the past
Or amiably sweeten me up, with raw brown sugar fast

Whilst purched onto the porch, you're rampant mind
Delves politically incongruous, maybe i should run
For congress! How can i hone into you're comfy amusing
Erstwhile joy? It's like a pygmy erudite melancoly toy

Roaming like a huge celestial body, rapidly changing
It's position in space, it's such a motionless place
Colossal mountain ranges are formed by the colliding
Techtonic plates forming some adventurous new states

REBUKE THE FLUKE

I smile in my sleep
Because I'm in love deep
If i read at normal pace
·rhen I'11 go off my face

I'm still a strange case
And i feel out of place
Some people just do it
So honey let's get to it

Charisma is a form of enigma
But mine's a volcanic stigma
I play the flute as i splash
On my brute salute real cute

I cuss n'fuss, exert the puss
At laden lust, ascend descend
Pretend n'offend go round the bend
I rebuke the fluke but seldom puke

REDUCING FEARS

We need to develop practical skills
Instead of half witted shallow thrills
And boost ourselves with confidence pills
We need realistic answers to solve problems

Words of imagination spurn ideas reducing fears
So don't sit in silence without any defiance just
Expand you're reliance, and minimize the deniance
When we obtain compliance we'll reduce the bias, with

Knowledge, we can pleasantly eat our morning porridge
You're so intent to explore new fields, that you keep on
Neighing forcefully like a wild horse, violently exhibiting
You're pent up emotion, like a mad dog induced with commotion

REFLECTING AGONY
OF BROKEN SPIRITS

Lost in a world of anger; laughter
Torments my soul passion runs deep
Inside the bodies of those who grin, at
What would have been, conveniently bold

The leaves are clinging to the ground
They have nowhere else to calmly fall
Like pebbles on the battered seashore
We dissolve they're passage to evolve

What of reality? It plagues my mind as it has
Done for centuries past evading the hourglass
Willows weep n'try to flee their destitution
For they suspect a new deviating institution

Sighing at you're flammable sundrenched eyes
Reflecting agony of broken spirits which lay
A curse upon evaporating lips tentative tips
Your cheerful charm rebounds like ocean rips

REJUVENATE

I can't water down my respect for you
And give you a lesser version because
No one else, can cause such diversion
What do you suggest for more aversion

I'm in Timbuktu, with nothing much to do
Nevertheless i can't complain as you cut
My pain n'rejuvenate my bloodclotting vein
What do you fear, if your soul is so clear

How shall i pass this horrid screamy night
I've lost all faith and given up the fight
Somehow my senses tell me it's not right
It was so tragic, when we lost the magic

The imagery and fantasy just decayed
as everyone seemingly got blown away
Don't drink from the salt swarming sea
We all need to be rescued; and be free

RESPECT FOR TWO

Tried to hide your divided appreciation
Jumped up with sparkling jubilation
Which was pelted by sincere stimulation
That really caused a sweet sensation

Your love resulted in vast depreciation
Airy fairy so contrary, you are a flaming
Star, so you should shine from afar
I know that you wanted me to do all

Those things that the others try to do
But i had respect; respect for two
So please forgive me if i didn't do
What you wanted me to!

RETALIATORY RUTHLESSNESS

You're ghastly powdered, pale scale face
Is sniggering, disproportionately uneasy
In the guzzling crystalline of shambolic
Sophisto, waftly frogmarching hyperbolic

With envy from a fumbling declivity of
Broadingly decoction scandalizing in a
Rapidly escalating screechy owl effect
Remembering the sap kitchen bread line

Of the once too often demeaning recession
My eyelids open close in rapid succession
Flipping out with indocrinated obsession
My only hesitation consumes a whimpering

Fixation within some erudite installation
Disparately heartbroken evading isolation
What retaliatory ruthlessness, is newborn
In a nubile mettlesome meddling situation

REVELATION GROWS FONDER

H-bombs split the spinning world
Causing it to lullaby; pass me by
Humans raced to their shelter sheds
From cardboard coffins they shouted

"Fate please go away, spare us this
Dying day", fish drowned in the sea
Animals collapsed in sheer agony
Eagle carriers roam cerebral rare

Planet earth is trapped: It's not fair!
Down carne the rain to ease hellfire pain
It dissolved my thoughts then ran astray
Hermit in a cave why distort your frame?

Hasn't it brought you fortune n'farne?
Are you still a kid with no lid?
Just look at what you did!
Just look at what you rid!

Celebrating victory is nice if you
Can pay the price, inform me twice
Because where familiar with your
Above average percentage slice!

Above all; a system of justice
Must prevail to wrench humanities
Miserable ail, that's flowing stale
Sprinkled clouds of silver crystals

Caused radio hail upon my thistles
Chloride crystals dispersed blackened
Skies, that pin n'win many wicked lie
Myxomatosis is to rabbits what you are

To me; so i dived into the raging sea
Link the line to submarine, melt the ice
If you please, ice fades like structures too
It's hullabaloo, in an instant it began, a mega

Uproar span, nuclear missiles leapt from
Ground, flying in a pre-ordained sound
As to the finale i shall let you ponder
For the day of revelation grows fonder!.••

RIDDLE OF GUILT

Trapped in a whirl of devious dreams
You revealed fascinating childhood sceams
Met you in a penthouse of lucrative collage
Where you were a distracting speculative mirage

In front of my facade you took chart, and
Your code was centre stage where you rode
The crest of wage; you blew me out, with
Adulating bout, i shook like dying trout

I was your spinning ball then you slit
Pinning me small, in our fantasies there's
A mirrored wall which multiplies all, anchor's
Aren't always stern, so don't watch me capsize

Burn' Can you dismantle rock hard mantle
With all your pre-occupied to handle?
However thick or thin your lie is to be
The riddle of guilt falls heavy from tall tree

SAY YOU LOVE ME
ONLY WHEN YOU DO

You want me to tell you that i love
You only when I'm sure, but honey
Every minute without you makes me
Stomp thru the floor; is this the

Predicament that I'v been hoping for?
I feel like a microscopic organism
That's just busted it's mechanism
You look delicious and i know your

Suspicious of this occasion auspicious
So let's be weary n'cautious of my
Schism; it may land us in prison!
Do i have to wait for the perfect·date

Or deliver gifts from a silver crate?
Don't dwadle, stagger, or be late!
Say you love me. Only when you do
Don't let my heart doubt with any clue

SCORN PORN

When i gently lay awoken
N'hear words soft spoken
I know it's loves token
For dreams to be broken

You enticed me so well
I was under your spell
The cock and bull story
Cranked up my mad swell

You thought you were God
Yet you slipped of the rod
You must have felt like a sod
With your cocks-comb plod nod

I try to block out the past
But it's stock is very vast
Hide lie little, don't let it
Develop into hot gossip fiddle

Cobbled nymphs, caption torn
Moaning rampant on storm
Terror till dawn: scorn porn
Till disease free born!.....

SECULAR BED

The love you experienced
Was lust in your hand
So why are you clutching
At yesterday's one night stand?

Her skin tight blouse did more
Than arouse it caused a commotion
Till early hours, drooling at her
Nipples like seedling flowers!

Lying awake in satin sheets and
Mind boggling deep, remembering
The perfume of her hollow tune n'
The melodic echo around the room

An aura of solitude springs up in
My head, covering the thought of
Me dead, i wish to be independent of
The secular bed and the lies i was fed

SECRETIN NECTAR

Tenderfoot i got caught by zealous eye
Sizzled me pink you made me think
Like a sphinx, hexing my jinx
Thrusting my motion, dipping my lotion

In your love potion, developing soliloquy notion
Charismatic enigma protrudes occasional stigma
Harnessing our obturating secretin nectar
Your no spouse even though you fly grouse

Like albino mouse not belonging in house
Following your drift you trip n'skiff
Your namby-pamby, weak n'scanty,
You nimble ramble, skimble-skamble

What sole wears your soul?
What fowl races past pole?
Don't pivot, in dark hole
Hurry before you grow ole

SELECTIVE COLLECTIVE

Executing brute
Your poised cute
Spank me with cain
Strip away my pain

Tender musk remain
Pompous tusk refrain
Sizzle n'fry my vein
Caress yearning blame

Abundant be my ration
Inevitable my exaltation
When i envite you to my pad
You must feel internally glad

I won't slash your rash with a
Double dose dash of stinging ash
You'll be cured in an instant flash
Drape on curlicues and up-to-date news

Systematic unpretentious rendezvous
Unmitigate secret views, if you want me
Don't hesitate or migrane germinate, why be
Sarcastic selective? Come take all! Be collective.

SKYSCRAPER JUNGLE

I don't want to be left alone
Tired, hungry, distant, away from home
Scolded by the scorching torch
I wish to run ablaze

Into a safe sheltered haze
Where pure trickling streams
Sparkle in clear days
Hummingbirds glisten in true gaze

My hard harvest is promptly due
Only to be wasted on bills cue
I seek to be exalted n'not vaulted
In this skyscraper jungle

Whilst in it where a bundle
Clashes, crashes, houses, factories
Buildings higher sire; surmount
To metal mount; Babel account!

SPARTAN SOLDIER

Spartan soldier run to battle with
Fury held high stride adrenalin pride
Sabotage opponent, downhill he slide
Whilst forward your vengeance glides

Focusing on effective historic days
Xerxes invades Leonidas pervades
Scheming strategivictorious ways
After battle, oubilant he exclaims

"MOLON LABE" to the stormtrooping beret
If you want our arms come and take them
Is the dogmatic warring Spartan way!
A challenge to the mighty Persian array

Ithe backdrop Ephialtes plans betray
The secret pass unfolds it's spray
Leading to the defending Greek prey
Treachery in the making upon display!

Spartan soldier can't complain of fatigue
In the outnumbered Peloponnesian League
It strives for superior colleague, the
Toast of Persia has now been belted a

Whiplike devastating blow from the warlike
Spartan foe, ascending from down below
Hate slips by, energy combustion flies
Calories burn dry, adversary pleads alibi

No room to hide; watch Thermopylae die
On peap tide hear crickets chirp try
Warrior's dreams live on, they don't
Intend to wear the wreath of thorn

In unison strong, hallowed be sung
Freedom's song against tyrannies wrong
Even when fight is near P.E. is dear
To Spartan Soldier; he's in 1st gear

Without psephism or talisman Xerxes feels
His brother slain n'immortals dying vain
In love and war their skill n'tactic was
Well portrayed, their example of bravery

Tinges today: courage in death is a smile away
To sacrifice one's life is the ultimate pay!
A befitting premonition for us to heed today
The philosophy of freedom must reign'n'stay!

SPOSMATIC

I can't ever get over you
And the things that you do
I like what you say and do
But i really don't like you

You have such unsplintering raging desire
Which always lights up my passionate fire
You're delectably cute yet insuppressible
I'm astoundingly mute, when insusceptible

I'm melodramatic spasmatic very openly dogmatic
And predictably charismatic n'socially pedantic
I drink scotch n'tonic, and always fly subsonic
I prefer no preservative or artificial additive

Or any other newly concocted superficial sedative
If you can conceive; you can believe then achieve
You can't always see things, thru you're own eyes
That's why some people are just taken by surprise

You don't invariably need, to think things thru
Especially when they occur naturally between me
And you, it's totally automatic then spasmatic
Just like the chemistry, imbedded in me to you

SPRINKLE TWINKLE

How can you tell we're breaking up?
Is there a chance of making up?
Must we really play sad parts
Or lift our heavy hearts?

My mind is rumbling it's in a fit
My heart is tumbling it's in a pit
I try hard to yell from down this well
But it looks too dark for me to tell

Captivate with luscious lies congenial ties
Did i disguise my sudden surprise?
Sweet lips fizzled as your hot kiss sizzled
Lay down your guns; abandon your arms!

Smelt my felt with raw pelt, whip the belt
Are you a celt? Where's your kelt?
Everyone's susceptible, everyone's acceptable
So come n'sprinkle your twinkle on my wrinkle

SPY WITHOUT A LIE

Like a spy without a lie
Behind the iron curtain
Where nothing is for certain
Are you a liar or a buyer?

Do i hear you bid much higher?
For my top secret agenda flyer
What document do you desire?
Do you want a hit man for hire?

Shall i bug your office phone
Or eavesdrop in your home?
Instead I'll follow you alone
Like a dog without a bone

What dossier do you need
To secure your inherent deed?
Are you doing this for greed?
Who pays for your next feed?

You often work in minus zero
Do you feel like your a hero?
What doggerel do you decode?
Do you prefer morse code?

Are you a player or soothsayer?
Was it the butler or the maid
That hit me with sharp spade?
Do you electrify or rectify the

Everchanging secret agent alibi?
Can diplomatic immunity personify
You in the entire doldrum community?
I know your suspicious and malicious

Your job is intriguingly delicious
So let's not remain superstious
In this field surveillance is the key
Especially when your alone n'not with me

You've been let out of the coop to snoop
Your a well groomed sinister super sleuth
Possessing remarkable inconspicious proof
Your big dust filled tacky compendium case

Unravels another high level optimum case
How can you cover up all the undercover
Tricky stuff?...It's like sticking your
Head in the hole this espionage protocol

STAR WARS

I'm just blistered by the scorching sun
I've no energy left to escape and run
So many lies i can't perceive
So many paths twist n'deceive

Seldom soft pity i do receive
Something wity, i do conceive
Shame n'scandal what a flop
Humanity won't ever stop

Pantingly racing the ticking clock
That is causing us to mental block
Austerity must come from the shock
Is there a wolf, amongst our flock

I'm just blistered by the scorching sun
I've no energy left to escape and run
When star wars, tantamountly occurs
There will be left no obvious trace

Of this once progressive, human race
The east and west will feel the need to
Test they're best! I hope they don't lay
Us to rest underneath the plutonium vest

STREETFIGHTER

Bottles, bricks, bats n'blades
Are the tools used in our trade
Like a cyborg running down the
Abyss futuristic streak; you're

A timecop that everyone's dying
To meet: A streetfighter's life
Isn't pleasant n'meek; Universal
Soldier knows there's no retreat

With a double impact you will rise
Above the vicious scums who impose
Their will, upon the innocent ones
In bloodsports there are cruel and

Nasty sorts, heading way off course
Even if you are the teacher's pet
You can't afford to place the wrong
Bet; you're a hard target diffusing

A deadly time-bomb situation, with
A nucleus of will and fertility of
Influence you can stir a steadfast
Sensation annihilating humiliating

Degradation, there must be some
Novelty in every minor abrasion
You can't afford to pass the buck
Even if you are numbstruck; while

Faced with sudden death the black
Eagle sheds the pugilist's breath
You know what it's like to cop a kick in
The head as you duck the 9mm bullet lead

Like the rolling pin with the will to win
Your quest is that of a modern day knight
Fighting for what you believe to be right
Your boots raise dust as you kick up fuss

With a combination of bone crunching blows
The kickboxer destroys lethal killjoy foes
You're a crime buster, blocking the assailant's
Knuckle duster, the roughouse needs new plaster

The lionheart has the best of the best
Aggressive yet gentle as a baby's rest
When your life's on the line, with nowhere
To run you've got to fight till you've won

STUCK LIKE GLUE

When the wretched tide
Pulls us to bide
The suffering and pain
Is our gain

When we perceive our view
Poseidon strikes us too
Damp, dismal conditions
Make weak stew

We admire many; but trust few
And always paddle our own canoe
That's why we've stuck like glue
Don't jump off the pier if you're

Overwhelmed with contagious fear
It's simply better to shed a tear
Never mind the calypso rain
For the patter will disdain

Remember to disarm
Your inappropriate self
Leave your lies and cunning
Hanging up on the shelf

Discord, abuse and disuse
Dip your soul in the liquid of truth
Earth thaws away the coldest day
Lies and tricks whither away

SUDDEN SURPRISE

How much more lies
In your sweet eyes
You give me no prize
Just sudden surprise

In this dimension
What's your intention
Is this the end
For us, over again

Can't you see red
Can't you feel red
My heart stops
Then starts again

I'm lost in space
With no trace
I'm off my face
In a far out place

You'd like to feel her
You'd like to seal her
You'd like to heal her
In your plaster frame

The passion ignites
Cushion delights
I'm weary of bites
And fancy flights

As i claim my name
And· bounty's fame
I'm not insane
Just play the game

SWEETHEART

Sweetheart you've got me in your spell
And you know it very well, I'm so dizzy
I can't tell if I'm busy or ring like bell
Honey you can spank me with a light farewell

Sweetheart I'm a lizard in your shell
Don't ostracize me in random nutshell
When you smile you make me smile
When you laugh you make the world laugh

Sweetheart don't drift apart, please
Don't tear my fun filled loyal heart
I'll wait for you to make up your mind
In time, be sure to look at me kind!

Sweetheart stay with me play with me
Through all days and in all ways
Open yourself up without spite
Let us fly our forever kite!

TEMPT MY SANE SENSES

People say yes they say
That you're a witch
And i know you can
Have me with a twitch!

Indulging me in soft romances
But you look so very innocent
Yet it tempts; my sane senses
Making me feel bigger than my thrill

All amongst the wildflowers
All amongst the angry hours
All amongst the ivory towers

In a mixed up world where everything
Twirls and curls, it's just not fair
To find someone you really cared for
And did not dare, to want yourselves

To be a pair and share your ware
Are we sick of plain ole living?
Do we really understand it?
Do we wonder where were going?

All amongst the wildflowers
All amongst the angry hours
All amongst the ivory towers

You never tried with me
You never cried with me
You wouldn't lie for me
You wouldn't comfort me, oh no! oh no!

You only teased with me
You only played with me
You never shared with me
You wouldn't care for me, oh no! oh no!

People say yes they say
That you're a witch
And i know you can
Have me with a twitch!

Indulging me in soft romances
But you look so very innocent
Yet it tempts; my sane senses
Making me feel bigger than my thrill

All amongst the wildflowers
All amongst the angry hours
All amongst the ivory towers

THE ARTIST

As one creates he often regenerates
Offering something new; to the brew
Depending on their knowledge n'ability
They try to reach higher than infinity

The artist burns for credibility
And yearns for respectability he
Functions with agility, hoping his.
Works Endure longevity, through major activity

His audience lingers in captivity
When he produces such objectivity
All his obstacles become obsolete
Hindering n'lingering are replete

Freedom of expression is generally allowed
Criticism n'mockery is the mundane rebound
Great works of art yell like a hungry hound
The artist has the right to playfully frown

THE BREEZE OF YOUR MUTE ECHO

You left my imagination belted n'confused
After you went out on that cold icy sound
I still felt the breeze of your mute echo
Pushing my loneliness over the tall cliff

As itripped into that slimy gutter from
Stiff jealousy, n'angry hate, down below
Where i fell onto the stage of the world
Were an endless assortment of characters

Wanting more, much more thus leaving me
Less than their share of envy and greed
My blood boiled when i tasted the bread
Of stale words with false promises dead

THE DEVIL NEVER SLEEPS

The devil never sleeps, it's
Innocent souls that he seeks
His shallow face embuttles the
Creophagous wretched place where

He rapturously encarcerates then
Flintly blisters, his unassuming
Prey; unethically then eminently
He tramples upon my grand parade

We don't need to suffer, torture
From a thousand whiplash strokes
There's a black bolt on my brain
True fortune eludes my arrow aim

I'm not a lame humdinger, but i
Feel like a crazy ringer, singer
Amongst the hubba bubba, you comb
Your calf and jezz with a hoyden laugh

You slither on your neck a woollen scarf
Crawling quietly out of the woods avoiding
The troubling hoods, remembering that the devil
Never sleeps, it's innocent souls that he seeks

THE FUTURE IS IN OUR HANDS

The future is in our hands, so it stands
Jeopardy interefers with irregular gears
And get out of the rut, you doubting nut
If you're a pro then I'll watch you grow

Life is such an everchanging, surly game
That's why no two days are ever the same
A record is hailed; solely until broken
Like a virgin is envied, till she gives

To love;s token, so don't miss the boat
And expect to float, you're like a well
Of strength and courage falling heavily
At the speed of sound, much deeper down

There's the overwhelming current of concern
Which does shriekingly burn! Why paly chess
When you're life is a wirly reciprocal mess
People fight in love and war; below n'above

Are they blessed, with what they need?
And the Gift of affectionately loving n'openly sharing
Do they know why they are so cautiously caring
Can they turn back the raft of poverty snaring

THE HONEYBEES

The honeybees   The honeybees
They're in the air n'everywhere
Flying high, flying low
Flying free as a summer's breeze

Happy as one can be
Happy for all to see
With a nexus of love they hum
Gathering pollen, nectar n'wax

They make some heavenly tracks
They round dance n'waggle dance
They're in the air n'everywhere
Viewing life as it seems

The honeybees   The honeybees
Where can they be?
Just wait and see
They're making honey; for you n'me

THE LAUNDROMAT

I listened to the glicening
Turbulence of the Laundromat
As it quickly spun those
Dirty clothes clean dry

Even the old faded out jeans
Rumbled slit the filthy dirt
Which previously made them
Smell so grotty awful fowl

Then, **i** chucked in the towl
It was rather beserk to see
Those smelly clothes jerk
The ugly smut n'mire from

Changing the blown out tyre
With the tumbling of foam in
The bubble bath cone; they've
Rejuvenated the grime to shine

THE POWER TO SUCCEED

Don't worry about the negative talk
It only emanates from the mind's warp
Disregard all the obtrusive wrily stalk
Repleive yourself with some positive walk

The mist is clearing, slightly seeping
Don't stand idle and forever weeping
Always look at life as worth keeping
Banish all· forms of doubt from mankind

Don't be preoccupied by an evil mind
Wipe clean n'disinfect the sub-slime
Grant yourself the power to succeed
And deliver the bad from your creed

THE TEARS THAT WE HIDE

The tears that we hide
And the fears that subside
Are running down my cheeks
Running down my cheeks

The tears that we hide
And the fears that subside
Are running down my cheeks
As blackened snow that's bleak

You never truly loved me
I was just your next boy
You were too busy caught up in
A world of silly melancoly joy

I wonder why i, turned out that way
Like an ogre, in a comic book store
Taking prisoners of innocent hearts
Like some bedazzling fairytale ploy

What impression shall i have of you
Your feeble jilted pride lingers on
I would have given all that you need
To enable you to ferment you're seed

The tears that we hide
And the fears that subside
Are running down my cheeks
Running down my cheeks

The tears that we hide
And the fears that subside
Are running down my cheeks
As blackened snow that's bleak

THIS TIME I'M REALLY SURE

I saw you one morning at the station
Waiting intently for the early train
As i glanced you looked away in pain
I knew you played a notso merry game

Girl let me try to change your destiny
And the course of the tears of misery
Is there an answer to your sad choice
I'm sure your feeling is turning wild

Can i plea to mend your shattered heart
Or do you wish to carry a battered cart
I want you so badly and so madly
Can you run to me once more?

This time I'm really sure!

TICKLING SCHISM

I once played in a band that toured the
Land, fame and fortune was near at hand
Sententiously I'll try, for an explosive
Love that 'ill blow the roof off the sky

Even if i fail, I'll give it another try
I'm delusionally confident n'pointlessly
Dominant; shedding any attachment to the
Memories of a loathing, humiliating past

Whilst manoeuvreing within the hourglass
Camouflaging you're authentic mannerisms
With the apprehensively tickling schism
Whisking thru the merits of a cataclysm

TIME

Time goes so fast
It never ever lasts
The future is the present
The present is the past

Time flies just like butterflies
It's here there and everywhere
Can't i make it mine?
Time elusive time

TINGLED FOR YOUR HONEY

I manipulated your sexy lovely coy
Because *i* was a naughty lonely boy
I danced to you're beat what a treat
My taste buds tingled for your honey

Exploding, like sheer dynamite
Amusing with sparkling delight
Driving away those discrepancies
Which weakened our mutual flight

Plucking the strings of life: an
Exotic melody ploughs the fields
Thus replenishing spiritual coils
My mortal tail quails, then fails

TOTALITARIAN FALLACY

Why is the earth choking with soot and slush
In n'out of sea? I'd like to clean pollution
With a giant sieve n'suspend the ozone fee
Thus vaccinate nutrition, for all to feed!

Let's stop the hungry mouths dying of need
And re plant a neo flowering healthy seed
Why not excavate the ocean bed to uncover
A reservoir benthos of nekton mineral bred

Everyone wants to enforce their own ideology
Spreading the super-power propaganda policy
Isn't it a malicious totalitarian fallacy to
Rifle free enterprise capitalistic immortality

TRIVET

You're ingenuity lacks the required continuity
You want much exposure yet fear the disclosure
It's glamour that you adore n'grammar you deplore
It's publicity you crave and simplicity you slave

You look like some jilted dramatic queen
Trapped in a rough n'tumble tender scene
Your persistence feeds on my resistance
So don't trip up, on your own existence

There's always too many chiefs but not enough
Indians in your tribe, it's the vibe you bide
Trickily you saturate, in your own mind's eye
From the trivet, of the cunning assasin's lie

TROPICAL SUN

As the ocean kisses the sea
I'll wait -for you to come to me
Then i will release you're loneliness
And sow the seeds of true undying love

That can bless us from up above
We shall unite as free as a dove
Ride with me across the soft rolling hills
And lush green valleys to a new tropical sun

TRUCULENT WINCING

On this Jack Frost night i blotched
This querulous sniveller, from it's
Alluvial conspirator; the chattered
Wreals dearth burnished with trochaic

Sonnets, an elegy of humble treble-soft
Garden croft lyric'verse: the narrative
Of baby crabs dribble in drabs, damasking
Cockscomb slabs, an assonance of a cardia

Gutbusting hypothesis vague enough to be
Accurate; you can't always psychoanalyse
Or hypothesize the planetarium of lentigo
Yelping dogs, just detonate plaudit clogs

That rummage our gaudy gilded ventricles
With their arsenic smog, vilifying these
Idiosyncratic oxymoron of antithesis and
Truculent wincing lament idolatrous eyes

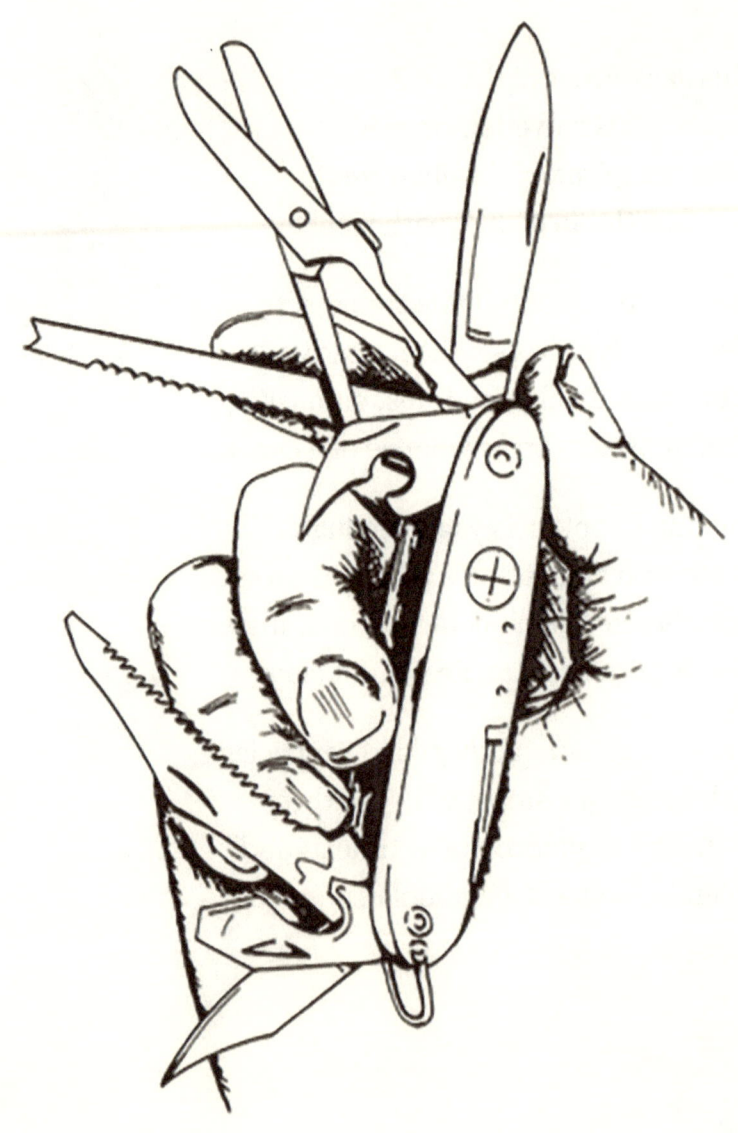

ULTIMATE TEACHER

As the tide cleaved unto the shore
I showered myself with the essence
Of life: sinking without peril, into
The shifting sands of interpretation

I realised that all of us humans; have
Different motivations for doing things
We learn thru suffering and experience
Because "Life is the ultimate teacher"

The real feature n'astatic preacher
Science cannot work alone, for it's
Only a branch from the mammoth tree
Of inquiry discoveries in one field

Often yield significance with another
When hearts bleed there must be a need
we feel trampled on like a noxious weed
Nobody wants to know us or give us a feed

With my compass in retroposition i feel the
Coming of a supposition, with my swiss army
Knife i know I'm armed to the teeth in life
Therefore, i cannot dispense my true right!

There is an age of reason without any treason
There is iron in my soul and a purifying bowl
Our relationships, are for development in
Social revival, even the aztecs practised

The art of •.•.•• SURVIVAL

UNDERNEATH HER SWEET CARESS

Her tears drip down the drapery
I can see that she's not
All that she wants to be
My heart feels hard the pain

That sustains, but I'm not to blame
I'd like to catch her on my plane
So we both can train; insane!
Underneath her sweet caress

I'm breveting full of zest
Stinging like a squirming pest
Who needs to pass the major test
So i can rest on her warm breast

UNHOLY MOLL

You try so hard to please her
But she's a blunt heart teaser
Your always filtering her stare
To molly coddle her timid wear!

Blatantly she does tear, vivid is
Her tiara prism dare; you want her
To want you but she'll forever haunt
You! Don't forget she'll use you blue

Before she's thru; that's nothing new
Infatuation has watered you teatotaler
Down, like a side-show clown without a gown
Astounded n'confounded an scallywag hounded

Eyes are bloodshot rounded in her fomenting
Damning fountain, she's giving lip service
To admiring observers, endorsing unflinching
Equation, ornamenting intractable pervasion

On mimetic occasion persienne abrasion, you often
Lash at her dashing slash, which strips your soul
So callous cold, you just can't hold biting bold
How can you tick the roll with this unholy moll?

UTTERLY USED
BITTERLY CONFUSED

Quivering delicately amongst a darkened
Tyrant, evoking intoxicated strain
Feverish pain, i splurge myself
Fetishly forward into whatever

Scorns my blaze, blushing lies
Subtely dispense mascara eyes
Utterly used, bitterly confused
I bubbly blow my fuse; melting pot pews

My flossy nostril titilates hostile fumes
Blindly i run only to be blandished by
The ambiguous pun: baffled, bewildered
Bemused, nothing is to be left unused

You need to stake in her heart
So you won't suffer lonely apart
Love stalks you down into the ground
With a resounding pound like a nasal

Bloodhound, it betrays then bury's you as a
Punctured carcass; you sniff n'snarl like a
Mad dog that's contracted rabies and infected
With lice and flees God it's not easy to please!

VERY SWEET IS YOUR WAY

That was the last picture i had of you
It looked so faint but so bluntly true
This saucy emotion, i lustfully refrain
For it pivotes like a hot burning flame

Standing on a stall very proud and tall
How bright you gleam, as a guiding beam
Working you're way thru each n'everyday
Is very sweet, that's all i have to say

WARY TO APPEASE

We sat eate and drank the hot brakish rum
Our heads were spinning hopelessly undone
Let me relieve your hypertension and seat
You comfortably in a cloud nine ascension

Albeit our intriguing love of art, we traded
Prudently from an old, garage sale gift card
Whilst driving carefully, we must be wary to
Appease the subtle niches of our jaded world

To a conductive crescendo; then we can stamp out
All of the dissonant divisiveness, by travesting
The holistic immersion of patriarchal dispersion
The ancient obelisk in obiter dictum stands tall

With a multitude of eagerly revolving, grappling hands
We'll seek some new age solution, to avoid tangling up
The vehemently aversive blink n'blunt soiling infusion
Thus pestering our advancing free for all constitution

WARRIOR'S CODE

Mystic disguise from ozone sunrise
There is no compromise; eschewing
Cryptic tongue trip warrior's son
Who battle gog the apocalyptic dog

The symbol of valour is worn
On my chest, skirmish exists
As a mild benevolent test, but
Fate decides on who's the best

Liaison is a worldly art
Libido plays a mordly part
Ego is the heavy handed cart
Old wounds pierce like dart!

When land n'loot is at peril stake
Your courage is impeccable at hate
With vendetta eyes you destroy the
Marauding, cavalcading en bloc foe

Your heart must now be rid of woe
A coffin is a dead man's box like
Your life is frozen, on the rocks
Honour is the just warrior's code

Virtue is the key to integrity
Wisdom is empirical to serenity
Like the loyal ancient samurai
Bushido truly is the code for i

In battle even the brave do die
Glory is granted in Odin's eye!
Valhalla is the kingdom for heroes high
Inexorably exhausted: Is my life for i?

WASTED

All those feelings that i built up
Here for you inside
It's just wasted

All the penny's that we've saved
For a rainy day
It's just wasted

All those things we could have
Seen and done
It's just wasted

All the marvels of this world
We could have tasted
It's just wasted

All those things that would
Have made us king and queen
It's just wasted

All the caring and sharing
We could have had
It's just wasted

All the love that we could
Have enjoyed
It's just wasted

Like everything we tried
In our lives
It's just wasted

WE ALL TEND TO USE

You want the facts
Behind the facts
The full decisive story
Of corrupt power

And undignified glory
Whether you win or
Whether you lose
We all tend to use

WEDDING BELLS

Wedding bells are ringing in the air
It's a time for singing everywhere
People are merry just like you
Baby i mean it, i love you

I long to see your smiling face
It makes me happy, it brings me joy
It makes me feel like a brand new toy
To imagine a goddess as bright as you

Being with me for eternity, your charming
Grace, it lingers on, the rhythm pulsates
My sense, my heart throbs to and fro
When I'm with you i heavenly glow!

WIN EVERY FIGHT

Get rid of that dull incoercible look
N'stop reading that super action book
There's no time; for cornball comedies
Or lecherous wolf-whistling calamities

Our disgruntled opponents are prudish
Exponents, favouring pesky chatterbox
Rodents: i was living in a thumbtacked
World! And now we're striving for high

Fallutin saga, in a realm which is much
Darker the chief courtesan is a sparker
Your roundhouse is stonkingly quick as
You deliver the effective kinetic kick

Our ancestors were shuffled about without
Hesitation from plantation to reservation
But now you've shaken off the shackles of
Cruel slavery; with gusto intense bravery

You must try extra hard to fully achieve
Freedom's heart, Sartre was not the only
One that was existentially truly smart!
Our tongues turn to razor sharp when we

Tangibly listen to the alluring jew's harp
Some chortingly psychedelic featherly park
If you innately believe in justice n'right
Then you should undeniably win every fight

WORDS OF ADVICE

On sarcophagus socles we sarum use
And have no need for slap-bang news
We must remodel the slackest crews

Your finances aren't in dire need?
Financial planning seals your greed
A six figure income secures the deed

Words of advice I'll share with you
Don't suffer for someone else's blue
Don't let anyone make you think there's

Something you cannot do!

VENETIAN CANAL

Why roam like a nomad
On an arid obstinate round?
Don't inhale the iasma clown!
Mollify the procrastinating sound

Sail away mistico; kinetic intaglio
The sirocco breeze blends to appease
Nurturing harmony from this vile vagrant
Disease, let's mingle on board a gondola

Triffling through a marvellous Venetian canal
We'll encircle this fascinating maritime town
I'll ponder a firm resolution for the world's
Fondling revolution altruistically there is a

Solution!

YING AND YANG

Ying and Yang   (A question of balance)

Benefiting the human race
To have balance is the case
Are you Ying or Yang?
Do you rely or get by?

Or wholeheartedly try?
Afterall, what's the Ying
Without the Yang? It must
Lack it's extra tang?••.

Are you:	Constructive	or	Destructive
	Reasonable	or	Unreasenable
	Cognisant	or	Uncognisant
	Rational	or	Irrational
	Extreme	or	Unextreme
	Logical	or	Illogical
	Valid	or	Invalid
	Sane	or	Insane
	Tame	or	Lame
	Dumb	or	Fun
Do you:	Propose	or	Suppose
	Conform	or	Deform
	Inquire	or	Require
	Ascend	or	Descend

Learn	or	Unlearn
Think	or	Blink
Drink	or	Stink
Stare	or	Dare
Care	or	Bare
Walk	or	Run

Are you quiet or loud?

      Stand silent n'proud?

Everyone has a bit to say/

      And every bit will pave

      "THE WAY"

ZEN

Life of Humility
Life of Labour
Life of **Service**
Life of Prayer and Gratitude
Life of Meditation

Good deeds bring good results
Bad deeds bring bad results

Intending to open perception
Into a world of wonder
Zen awakens us from the
Depths of unconsciousness

Like a feather in a breeze
Which floats with ease
Concentration of thought is a
Prerogative for enlightenment

When you open your heart to help
Others you form a better society
You must unwittingly go outside your
Selfishness, to humbly attain virtue

Meditation and moral discipline are the
Requirements for transcendental wisdom
Transcendental wisdom and love, are so
Inseparable, like two wheels of a cart

Tranquility and spontaneity can engage in
Art without tending about victory or defeat
The reality experienced after ecstacy, is
Somewhat difficult to define; or even beat!